LIES RELIGION TAUGHT ME

and

THE TRUTH THAT SET ME FREE

BY

CONNIE WITTER

D0931599

Lies Religion Taught Me and The Truth That Set Me Free
ISBN: 978-0-578-42452-1
Copyright © 2018 by Because of Jesus Publishing
P.O. Box 3064
Broken Arrow, OK 74013-3064

Cover Design by: Nancy Bishop
nbishopsdesigns.com

Editing and Interior Design by: Yattira Editing Services
contact@yattira.com

Printed in the United States of America.

Acknowledgements

I especially want to thank the staff of
Because of Jesus Ministries:

Marsha Rivers: Office Administrator

Gwen Myrie: Office help; Social Media; Women of Grace
Speaker

Lisa Aldrich: Web Design Administrator

Sherry Hensley: Marketing; Conference MC

Shannan Orr: Book Sales; Marketing; Women of Grace
Speaker

Thank you all for reading through the Bible study each
week and giving me your honest opinions and feedback
on each chapter. You helped me get this book finished,
and I am forever grateful for your friendship, love, and
support! I love and appreciate you all very much!

Table of Contents

Note from the Author

This book is my personal journey out of performance-based religion into the freedom found in Jesus and His amazing grace! In each chapter of this study, I share a lie religion taught me, and the truth about Jesus that set me free! At the end of each chapter are questions that will inspire you to reflect on what was taught.

I encourage you to ask the Holy Spirit to reveal the truth to you in each one of these areas where religion has kept you bound. Jesus said the Holy Spirit was sent to point you to Him and guide you into all truth! (John 16:13).

As you read through each chapter, simply ask the Holy Spirit to open the eyes of your understanding so that you can see Jesus and all that He has done for you. I pray that the truth about Jesus will set your heart free from any fears, or feelings of inadequacy, that have been created in your heart by the lies religion has taught you. Jesus came to set you free from performance-based religion. You can live free in His Perfect Love!

Not simply for personal use, this book can also be beneficial for a group study. Gather a few of your friends, read each chapter, and discuss the questions together. Iron sharpens iron, and you can help one another gain even more insight into the truth that sets us free! (Proverbs 27:17, John 8:32).

In addition, the video and audio teachings of each chapter can be found on my personal ministry website at www.conniewitter.com. They are free of charge, and I encourage you to really delve into what the Lord wants to reveal to your heart about the freedom you have in His love for you!

Real People! Real Freedom!
What Others Are Saying About This Teaching

"Thank you, Connie! I believe there is hope for me after legalistic brainwashing and fear producing sermons. Let's sink the ship of religion together. Bless you, Connie Witter. You provide oxygen to my soul. I'm coming up for air." — Jennifer

"Wow! This is really revelation time!! This teaching helped me to become free from the judgmental thinking I had." — Blom

"The Lord's timing is always perfect. Last week, after starting this Bible study, I received a call that my Mom had passed on. If I wasn't drinking from grace, if I wasn't believing that because of Jesus all is well with me, I would have done what I have been doing for the past 20 years of my 'Christian walk': "Melissa, you did not pray enough. Melissa, if you were walking after the spirit you should have discerned this." When that accusing voice came, I just thanked the Lord for His love for me, for His Grace and Peace, and for JESUS!!! Condemnation, you have been Terminated! You can't touch this Girl! Woohoo!!!" — Melissa

"FEAR! I have fought it all my life! This teaching is bringing me so much JOY and PEACE! I needed this so badly. Thank you, Jesus!" — Marianne

"Religion only taught me fear, guilt, and condemnation, but now I'm experiencing freedom in Christ Jesus!! Woohoo!" — Mary

"This is such a good message, given with such clarity and joy. I love how you focus not just on the negative (we are not under the tithe) but on the joy of being delivered into true joyful generosity that can only come by faith and love through the leading of the Holy Spirit. Loved it!" — Pastor Greg Riether, Healing Grace Church, Tulsa, OK

"I am grateful for New Covenant teachers like Connie Witter who continue to tell the world the Good News about Jesus!" — Buntu

"So thankful for the truth that is setting me free!" — Stephanie

"I receive every revelation, Connie! My spirit bears witness because now I feel free to tithe and give because I'm loved, versus feeling condemned when I don't give or tithe! I feel a weight lifted from my shoulders. Thank you, Jesus for setting me free! Hallelujah!" — Kawana

"My daughter and I have been listening to your teachings each day and then discussing them at night and each time we find more and more freedom! So thankful for you and love you lots." — Elaine

"Sister, this has freed me! Thank you, Jesus! I was going into debt while tithing. I was thinking I had to pay for God's blessings. Thank you for shedding light in the truth of God's Word." – Nicolette

"Thank you, a million times, for speaking the truth about 1 John 1:9. This truth set my family and I free. We are never going back! This revelation of complete forgiveness has transformed every aspect of my life in a positive way. It is ALL because of Jesus! Woohoo!!" — Sandra

"Connie, this teaching is so clear, so powerful, so freeing!!" — Judy

"I was always sin conscious, but not anymore! I am Jesus conscious now." — Monica

"WOW! What happiness!! Never ever does my good, good Father hold my mistakes against me!" — Sherry

"My heart no longer condemns me. I no longer condemn others." — Heather

"I was under the bondage of believing I don't have enough faith! Jesus has all the faith I need!" — Cindy

"I asked the Father to establish me in His righteousness, and I stumbled across your teaching, and it so helped me understand the Father's love for me and His heart toward me." — Yvonne

"This has got to be one of my favorite teachings by you. I love everything you said. I just think it's such a life transforming Truth for us as individuals, but then for us as mothers and fathers to take this Truth of who we are as children of God, then parenting out of that Truth and learning how to address the hearts of our children, rather than focusing on behavior modification. Disciplining out of compassion rather than out of punishment or condemnation." — Elise

"I had been believing the lie that if I didn't tithe I would be cursed by God. Of course, this produced fear in my heart, just like Connie teaches will happen when we are trying to live under the old Covenant law. But something very profound shifted and produced great joy in me when I decided to stop believing the lie that I could in some way qualify myself for God's blessing and instead became 100% convinced that I am blessed because of Jesus alone!" – Sandra McCollom, Founder of Freedom Living Ministries and author of *I Tried Until I Almost Died!*

Chapter 1
The Lie Religion Taught Me About God's Judgment

When I was growing up in church, I heard people teach that when I stand before God at the end of my life, I will be judged for all the things I've done wrong. It was explained to me that, like a movie, my life would be displayed for all to see. Have you ever heard someone teach that?

I remember when someone would teach this subject, they would use a scripture in the Bible, so it was easy to convince my heart that it must be true. This teaching produced fear in my heart. I can remember thinking, *I don't want to see Jesus if I have to publicly account for all that I've done wrong.* The sad thing about being taught this lie is that the Gospel is supposed to be Good News, and that isn't Good News at all!

Yet, for years, I did not question that belief because I thought, *If it came from the Bible, it must be true!* During preparation for this Bible study on the lies religion taught me, I visited with many people who had believed this same lie and had developed fears that were similar to mine.

The Truth That Set Me Free!

The inspiration to write this book came one day while I was reading 1 Corinthians 1:7-9. As I read this passage of Scripture, I recalled that lie I used to believe. That day, I also remembered the truth that set me free from the lie and how it has forever brought peace to my heart!

1 Corinthians 1:7-9 tells us the truth of what happens when we stand before our Heavenly Father in Christ:

> *"7...while you wait and watch [constantly living in hope] for the coming of our Lord Jesus Christ and [His] being made visible to all.*
>
> *8And He will establish you to the end [keep you steadfast, give you strength, and guarantee your vindication; He will be your warrant against all accusation or indictment so that you will be]* **guiltless** *and* **irreproachable** *in the day of our Lord Jesus Christ.*
>
> *9God is faithful (reliable, trustworthy, and therefore ever true to His promise,*

and He can be depended on); by Him
you were called into companionship and
participation with His Son, Jesus Christ
our Lord" (AMPC, emphasis mine).

We may need to read through these verses more than once to fully grasp what God has really promised us through Jesus. It is incredibly Good News! These scriptures say that Jesus will establish you to the end. He'll keep you steadfast, give you strength, and guarantee your vindication. He will be your warrant against all accusation and indictment, and you will be guiltless, innocent, and irreproachable on the day of our Lord Jesus Christ. Then, in verse nine, it says that God is faithful, and He will do exactly what He has promised you! Now, that is the kind of Good News that makes your heart happy and frees you from all fear!

Now, as I was reading this passage of Scripture, the word that stood out to me was "irreproachable." I thought, *What does it mean to be irreproachable before God?*

Irreproachable: beyond criticism, faultless, impeccable, blameless, flawless, outstanding, exceptional, admirable, and perfect. (www.dictionary.com/browse/irreproachable).

These words describe our identity in Jesus! Let's read 1 Corinthians 1:8 again, with this definition in mind:

"He will establish you to the end. He will keep you steadfast, give you strength, and guarantee your vindication. He will be your warrant against all accusation and indictment so that you will be guiltless and irreproachable—beyond criticism, faultless, impeccable, blameless, flawless, outstanding, exceptional, admirable, and perfect in the day of our Lord Jesus Christ."

Take a moment to think about these words and how your Good Father sees you—both now and forever in Christ! If this is the truth, do we have anything to fear when we stand before Him? Absolutely not! Perfect Love has chosen to see us as perfect because of Jesus!

There are so many scriptures in the Bible that confirm this Good News:

Hebrews 8:12 tells us that our Good Father will never remember our sins.

> *"For I will forgive their wickedness and will remember their sins no more"* (NIV).

Hebrews 10:14 tells us that by His one and final sacrifice, Jesus made us perfect forever.

> *"For by one sacrifice He has made perfect forever those who are being made holy"* (NIV).

Ephesians 1:4:

> *"Even before he made the world, God loved us and chose us in Christ to be holy and without fault in his eyes"* (NLT).

When you really believe and embrace this truth, no one will ever be able to deceive you with religious lies about God's judgment another day in your life. No one will be able to put you in bondage to fear of judgment ever again. You will live forever free, knowing that you are perfect, holy, and without fault in your Father's eyes, because of Jesus!

You have God's promise, and He is faithful, reliable, and dependable. If He says you are outstanding, flawless, faultless, and innocent, then that's what is true about you. Plus, He will be your warrant against all accusations to the contrary.

What does it mean that Jesus will be your warrant against all accusations? Usually, warrant is a word that can cause fear. However, let's take a look at this word, and discover what it really means:

Warrant: 1. authorization, sanction, or justification; 2. something that serves to give reliable or formal assurance of something; guarantee, pledge, or security; 3. something considered as having the force of a guarantee or as being positive assurance of a thing. (www.dictionary.com/browse/warrant?s=t)

Jesus is your guarantee that no one will ever be able to accuse you before the Father. He is your justification. He is your pledge and security against all accusations! You are who your Father says you are, and Jesus is your positive assurance—with the force of a guarantee—that no other voice has the power to accuse you otherwise! You are secure in your Father's Perfect Love!

Where Did This Religious Lie Come From?

If the truth is that you stand before your Good Father guiltless and irreproachable in His sight, that

Jesus is your warrant against all accusation, and you are now and forever faultless, beyond criticism, blameless, flawless, outstanding, exceptional, admirable, and perfect in Christ, then where did the lie that you will be judged for what you've done wrong come from? Why do so many people in the church still believe that God is judging them for their sins? Why do so many live in guilt and fear, if Jesus came to set us free?

As I stated earlier, the reason I believed those lies is because someone used a scripture to convince me that God would judge me for my sins and failures. It's true that if you look up the word "judgment," you will find a lot of judgment scriptures in the Bible. If you're familiar with the Bible, you may even be thinking of one of those judgment scriptures right now.

But I have Good News for you! Those judgment scriptures don't apply to you. Just because you read a verse in the Bible does not mean it applies to you. Let me explain: In Deuteronomy 28:1-67, the Bible lists the blessings and the curses of the law. These verses state that if you obey the law, you will be blessed, but if you disobey the law, you will be cursed. Well, we all know that all of us have disobeyed the law, so that would place us all under the curse of the law. But, that's not the end of the story. Thank you, Jesus! The Good News about what Jesus did for us is found in Galatians 3:13-14:

> *"13Christ purchased our freedom [redeeming us] from the curse (doom) of the Law [and its condemnation] by [Himself] becoming a curse for us, for it is written [in the Scriptures], Cursed is everyone who hangs on a tree (is*

*crucified); ¹⁴To the end that through
[their receiving] Christ Jesus, the
blessing [promised] to Abraham might
come upon the Gentiles, so that we
through faith might [all] receive [the
realization of] the promise of the [Holy]
Spirit"* (AMPC).

Jesus purchased your freedom from the curse of the law by becoming a curse for you. Now, through faith in Jesus, you have become an heir of the blessing. You are a joint heir with Jesus to all the blessings of God. Because of Jesus, the curses listed in Deuteronomy 28:15-67 do not apply to you! You have been set free from the condemnation of the law.

Romans 3:19 says, "Now we know that whatever the law says, it speaks to those who are under the law..." (AMPC). This verse says that whatever the law says, it is only speaking to those who are under the law. So, to know if those scriptures apply to you, you have to ask and answer the question, "Am I under the law, or am I in Christ?"

Romans 6:14 answers that question:

"For sin shall no longer be your master, **because you are not under the law, but under grace"** (NIV, emphasis mine).

The Good News is that because of Jesus, you are not under the law. So, all those scriptures, which talk about the condemnation and judgment that comes from disobedience to the law, don't apply to you! You are under God's grace! So, when a religious teaching uses a scary scripture to try to convince you of God's judgment, you can simply say, "I am in Christ Jesus! Those verses don't apply to me. I am not under the law, I am under God's grace, because of Jesus!

When you are free from this lie of religion, teachers of the law can't use those scary judgment scriptures to control you with fear anymore. When you know who you are in Christ, you'll no longer be deceived by judgment scriptures that don't apply to you.

What Did Jesus Say?

Let's look at what Jesus said about God's Judgment:

John 3:16-17:

> *"16For this is how much God loved the world—He gave his one and only, unique Son as a gift. So now everyone who believes in Him will never perish but experience everlasting life. 17God did not send his Son into the world to judge and condemn the world, but to be its Savior and rescue it!"* (TPT).

John 3:18:

> *"He who believes in Him [who clings to, trusts in, relies on Him] is not judged [he who trusts in Him never comes up for judgment; for him there is no rejection, no condemnation..."* (AMPC).

Jesus told us very clearly in these verses that God did not send Him to condemn or to judge the world.

God sent Him to *save* the world. Jesus said that God sent Him to rescue you from the condemnation of the law. 2 Corinthians 3:6 tells us that the law condemns and kills you, but the Spirit gives you life.

If you have put your trust in Jesus, the law has lost its power to condemn you. Jesus said that whoever believes in Him is not judged. He who trusts in Him will never come up for judgment. There is no condemnation for those who are in Christ Jesus (Romans 8:1). When you believe Jesus, and accept His gift of righteousness, there is no more judgement, condemnation, or fear of rejection for you. Jesus said it, and Jesus is not a liar! What He says is the truth!

Perfect Loves Casts Out All Fear of Judgment

1 John 4:16-18:

> "16We have come into an intimate experience with God's love, and we trust in the love he has for us. God is love! Those who are living in love are living in God, and God lives through them. 17By living in God, love has been brought to its full expression in us so that we may fearlessly face the day of judgment, because all that Jesus now is so are we in this world. 18Love never brings fear, for fear is always related to punishment. But love's perfection drives the fear of punishment far from our hearts. Whoever walks constantly afraid of punishment has not reached love's perfection" (TPT).

Isn't that one of the most beautiful passages of Scripture you have ever read? When you trust in God's Perfect Love for you, love is brought to its full expression in you, because as Jesus is, so are you in this world. This is so that you will be fearless on the day of judgment.

Love never brings fear to your heart, and fear is always related to punishment. God's Perfect Love drives the fear of punishment far from your heart. If we're still afraid of judgment, then we have not fully received and understood how much we are loved.

Jude 1:24 says, *"Now to Him Who is able to keep you without stumbling or slipping or falling, and to present [you] unblemished (blameless and faultless) before the presence of His glory in triumphant joy and exultation [with unspeakable, ecstatic delight]"* (AMPC).

Now, that's what Perfect Love looks like. Can you believe you're loved like this? Your Good Father looks at you in the middle of your failures and reminds you of what *He* sees. While the law would judge you and condemn you guilty, Jesus presents you blameless and faultless in the Father's presence. In the middle of your failure, He looks at you through the eyes of Perfect Love and says, *"My beloved child, you are guiltless and irreproachable in my sight. You are faultless, blameless, flawless, outstanding, exceptional, admirable, and perfect in Christ. You are my greatest delight! Your behavior will never change who you are or what I see when I look at you."*

When you embrace His Perfect Love for you and believe what Jesus did for you in his death, burial, and resurrection, you will live fearless in this world. You will run to your Good Father, without any fear of judgment, because you know that all you're going to experience is His perfect, unfailing, and unchanging love!

I so love sharing the Good News. I can't tell you how many times I've read these scriptures, and every single time it makes me fall in love with Jesus all over again. The truth has set me free from the religious lie that I'm going to be judged for my failures and sins.

I pray that you will join me and live in the freedom that Jesus came to give you. The devil used scriptures to try and deceive Jesus, and He is still using scriptures through religion to deceive God's beloved children today.

Remember, the Law speaks to those who are under the law. You are not under the law. You live in the freedom of God's grace. So, the next time one of those scary judgment scriptures is presented to you, remember to simply say, "That doesn't apply to me! Jesus set me free! I am guiltless and irreproachable in my Father's eyes, because of Jesus! Perfect Love has driven the fear of punishment far from my heart! I am loved!"

REFLECTION AND DISCUSSION QUESTIONS FOR CHAPTER I

1. Have you ever been taught that you would have to account for all the things you've done wrong when you stand before God? How did that make you feel?

2. How did you feel when you read the truth found in 1 Corinthians 1:7-9? What are your thoughts on the definitions of irreproachable and Jesus being your warrant against all accusations? How does your Good Father see you in Christ?

3. How does Hebrews 8:12, Hebrews 10:14, and Ephesians 1:4 further confirm the truth about how your Good Father sees you in Christ?

4. Did judgment scriptures that have previously put fear in your heart come to your mind when you read this chapter? According to Romans 3:19 and Romans 6:14, why do these verses no longer apply to you?

5. There are many verses in the Bible that describe the judgment or curse of the law, but what does Galatians 3:13-14 tell you Jesus did to set you free?

6. Make John 3:16-17 personal. What did Jesus say about you in these verses? How does this truth make your heart feel?

7. According to 1 John 4:16-18, Who is God? Will you ever be afraid of judgment if you believe God truly loves you? Why can you be fearless on the day of judgment? What does God's Perfect Love drive far from your heart? How does this truth set you free?

Chapter 2
The Lie Religion Taught Me About God's Judgment Toward Unbelievers

In the last chapter, we discussed the lie religion taught me about God's judgment toward those who believe. We discovered the truth that there is no judgment, no condemnation, and no accusations toward those who are in Christ Jesus.

But what about those who haven't believed? How does our Good Father feel toward them? Religion has taught the lie that God is angry and judgmental toward those who sin. I'm sure all of us have heard those messages where someone has taught that God is judging America because of people's sins.

However, that is exactly the opposite of what Jesus teaches us about our Good Father. So today, instead of listening to religious lies about our Good Father, let's listen to Jesus. He is the Truth about the Father, and the truth sets our hearts free!

The Truth About Our Good Father is Found in Jesus

John 1:17-18 says, *"¹⁷For while the Law was given through Moses, grace and truth came through Jesus Christ. ¹⁸No man has ever seen God at any time; **the only unique Son**, or the only begotten God, Who is in the bosom [in the intimate presence] of the Father, He has declared Him [He has revealed Him and brought Him out where He can be seen; He has interpreted Him and He has made Him known]"* (AMPC, emphasis mine).

Let's read these verses again in the Passion Translation:

> *"¹⁷Moses gave us the Law, but Jesus, the Anointed One, unveils truth wrapped in tender mercy. ¹⁸No one has ever gazed upon the fullness of God's splendor except the uniquely beloved Son, who is cherished by the Father and held close to his heart. Now he has unfolded to us the full explanation of who God truly is!"*

You will never find the truth about the Father by reading the Old Covenant Law. These verses tell us so clearly that Jesus came to unveil the truth about the Father. He has unfolded to us the full explanation of who God truly is! We don't have to wonder or question His heart toward people anymore. It's no longer a mystery what God is like. All we do is look at Jesus, and we'll see our Good Father in the face of Jesus Christ. In John 14:9 Jesus said, *"Anyone who has seen Me has seen the Father"* (AMPC).

Jesus is the express image of the Father. He has declared Him. He has revealed Him and brought Him out where He can be seen. He has made Him known.

The Law Blinds Us, But Jesus Makes Us See

The law blinds people from the true character of God, but Jesus makes us see!

2 Corinthians 3:14-17:

> *"14But [in fact] their minds were hardened [for they had lost the ability to understand]; for until this very day at the reading of the old covenant the same veil remains unlifted, because it is removed [only] in Christ. 15But to this day whenever Moses is read, a veil [of blindness] lies over their heart; 16but whenever a person turns [in repentance and faith] to the Lord, the veil is taken away. 17Now the Lord is the Spirit, and where the Spirit of the Lord is, there is liberty [emancipation from bondage, true freedom]. 18And we all, with unveiled face, continually seeing as in a mirror **the glory of the Lord**, are progressively being transformed into His image from [one degree of] glory to*

> *[even more] glory, which comes from the Lord, [who is] the Spirit"* (AMPC, emphasis mine).

These verses explain that even until this very day, when people read the Old Covenant Law, a veil is on their eyes and they have lost the ability to understand. The law blinds people from the truth about the Father. The veil is only removed in Christ. When a person turns to Jesus, the blindness is removed, and they experience true freedom. When we look to Jesus, the veil is lifted, and we see the glory of the Father. We clearly see His character and Who He truly is! God is Perfect Love! (1 John 4:16-19).

I read the Bible for a long time with a veil over my eyes. I was blinded because I was reading the Scriptures through the lens of the law. When I read the Scriptures through the lens of the law, I misunderstood them. I didn't see the Father clearly. But when I turned to Jesus, I finally saw the glory of the Father. Jesus revealed the Father's Perfect Love for me, and it set my heart free from fear and condemnation.

In Luke 9:35, the Father said, *"This is my beloved Son, Whom I have chosen; listen to Him!"* (NIV). So, if you want to know the truth about the Father, listen to Jesus!

In John 3:16-18, Jesus said:

> *"16God so greatly loved and dearly prized the world"* (AMPC).

> *"16For this is how much God loved the world—he gave his one and only, unique Son as a gift. So now everyone who*

believes in him will never perish but experience everlasting life. ¹⁷God did not send his Son into the world to judge and condemn the world, but to be its Savior and rescue it!

¹⁸So now there is no longer any condemnation for those who believe in him, but the unbeliever already lives under condemnation because they do not believe in the name of God's beloved Son" (TPT, emphasis mine).

Religion often paints the Father as an angry God, who judges and condemns sinners. But in John 3:16, Jesus told us that the Father greatly loves and dearly prizes every human being. And in Verse 17, Jesus clearly revealed the Father's heart for the world when He told us, "The Father did not send Me into the world to condemn or pass judgment on the world, but to be its Savior and rescue it!"

The Father sent Jesus to save us from the condemnation of our own sins. The law pointed out our failures and condemned us. The law told us we weren't good enough. But Jesus came to tell us, "You are greatly loved and dearly prized. I highly value you! I gave my life for you to prove my great love!" Jesus invited you to find your life and your identity in Him.

In John 3:18, Jesus said, *"...The unbeliever already lives under condemnation because they do not believe in the name of God's beloved Son"* (TPT).

If God Doesn't Condemn, Then Where Does it Come From?

So, if God is not condemning and judging unbelievers, where does the condemnation and judgment come from? Let's look at what Jesus said, in John 5:22 & 24:

> *"22Even the **Father judges no one**, for He has given all judgment (the last judgment and the whole business of judging) entirely into the hands of the Son... 24I assure you, most solemnly I tell you, the person whose ears are open to My words and believes and trusts in Him Who sent Me has eternal life. And he does not come into judgment [will not come under condemnation], but he has already passed over out of death into life"* (AMPC).

Remember what the Father said in Luke 9:35, *"This is my beloved Son, Whom I have chosen; Listen to Him!"* Did you listen to what Jesus said about the Father in John 5:22? Jesus said, ***"The Father judges no one!"*** In this verse, the Greek word for judge means "to condemn; to punish; to judge" (Strong's G2918). So, Jesus was actually saying, *"The Father condemns, punishes, and judges no one!"*

In John 5:22, Jesus went on to say that the Father gave all judgment into the hands of the Son. Isn't that an interesting scripture? Religion has taught us that the Father is an angry, condemning, judgmental God, and Jesus saved us from God's judgment. But Jesus, the Truth, said that the Father condemns, punishes and judges no one, and that the Father **gave all judgment to Him**.

Then in John 5:45, Jesus speaks to those who are unwilling to come to Him, so they might have life:

> *"Put out of your minds the thought and do not suppose [as some of you are supposing] that I will accuse you before the Father.* ***There is one who accuses you—it is Moses,*** *the very one on whom you have built your hopes [in whom you trust]"* (AMPC, emphasis mine).

Now, remember, Jesus said the Father judges no one, but He's given all judgment to the Son. Then He went on to say, "Don't even let the thought enter your mind that the Father or the Son is the One judging you. It's not, I, who judges you. **It's the law of Moses that judges and condemns you**." 2 Corinthians 3:6 tells us that the law condemns and kills, but the Spirit gives life!

What About the Wrath of God?

If it's true that the Father is not judging anyone, and Jesus isn't judging or condemning anyone, then what about all those verses on the wrath of God?

Remember, God is love, and every emotion and action comes out of His Perfect Love for us. If God is love, then the wrath of God is the wrath of love. If we want to fully understand the truth about the anger of God, we must look at Jesus. He is the express image of the Father. When you see what Jesus is angry about, you see what the Father is angry about.

Jesus said when you see me, you see the Father. So, let's look at three times in the Gospels where we find instances when Jesus was angry.

In Mark 3:1-6, Jesus had broken the religious law of the Pharisees by healing a man with a withered hand on the Sabbath day, so they were upset. Jesus became angry because their religious system **kept those He loved from coming to Him to be healed and made whole.**

In Mark 10:13-16, we see that Jesus was angry because the disciples wouldn't let the little children, **whom He loved**, come to Him.

In Matthew 21:12-14, Jesus got angry and turned over the tables of the money changers because the religious leaders were telling people they had to pay for God's forgiveness when **forgiveness was a free gift in Him**.

Again, we see God's wrath is not toward sinners, but rather toward a religious system that keeps those He loves from receiving His free grace and His unconditional love!

Mark 2:15-17 tells us that Jesus sat with sinners and was their friend, and the religious leaders judged Him for it! Not once in Scripture did Jesus condemn, judge, or punish someone for living in sin, or acting badly. Jesus showed us very clearly that **the Father's anger is against anything that keeps those He loves from experiencing His Life.** Every time Jesus displayed any type of anger in the Gospels, it was when He encountered the teachers of the law.

Not only was He angry at the religious system that robbed the people of experiencing His Life, but He was also grieved for the religious teachers themselves. The hardness of their hearts kept them from personally receiving His gift of eternal life.

Jesus loves the teachers of the law, but He is angry at their religious teaching that produces fear and condemnation in the hearts of those He loves (Matthew 23:13).

Jesus Revealed the Father's Heart Toward Those Caught in Sin

There is not one record in the Gospels of Jesus being angry or judgmental toward those caught in sin. It's actually quite the opposite! In John 8:3-5, 7, & 9-11, we clearly see the true heart of the Father as we look at Jesus, when He shows mercy and compassion, instead of judgment:

> *"3 When the scribes and Pharisees brought a woman who had been caught in adultery. They made her stand in the middle of the court and put the case before Him.*
>
> *4Teacher, they said, This woman has been caught in the very act of adultery. 5Now Moses in the Law commanded us that such [women—offenders] shall be stoned to death. But what do You say [to do with her—what is Your sentence]?"*
>
> *"7...Let him who is without sin among you be the first to throw a stone at her."*

"9They listened to Him, and then they began going out, conscience-stricken, one by one, from the oldest down to the last one of them, till Jesus was left alone, with the woman standing there before Him in the center of the court.

10 ...He said to her, Woman, where are your accusers? Has no man condemned you? 11 She answered, No one, Lord! And Jesus said, I do not condemn you either. Go on your way and from now on sin no more" (AMPC).

These verses tell the story of a woman caught in adultery. The religious leaders threw her before Jesus and said, "We caught this woman in the arms of a man who is not her husband! The Law says she must be stoned to death! So, what is your judgement call?"

Jesus looked at those religious leaders that were condemning her with the law and said, "How about this? Whoever among you has never broken the Law—whichever among you is perfect—you throw the first stone at her. Then the rest can join in, okay?"

Every one of them dropped their stones because according to the Law they were all guilty of sin. There was only One person there who was perfect—and they didn't qualify!

Then Jesus looked at that woman through the eyes of the Father, through the eyes of Perfect Love and said, "Where are those who wanted to kill you for your sin? Were any of those men perfect?" She replied, "No one, Lord." Then Jesus—the only One who would have qualified to judge her—said, "I don't condemn you either. Go and sin no more."

In that moment, Jesus rescued her from the condemnation of the law. She was now free to live from the identity that Jesus had offered her. She was free to find her life in Him. In the middle of her sin, Jesus looked at her through the eyes of Perfect Love and gave her loving kindness and grace. Jesus was revealing the very heart of the Father toward all who are caught in sin.

See, the law was condemning that woman, but Jesus came to rescue her from the condemnation of the law. Jesus was demonstrating the truth of what He had taught us about the Father in John 5:22-45. The Father judges no one. He has left all judgment to the Son. In John 5:45 Jesus said, "Don't even let it enter your mind that I am the one who judges and accuses you. It's the Law of Moses that condemns and judges you!"

And in John 8:15, while continuing to address the religious leaders, Jesus said, *"15You [set yourselves up to] judge according to the flesh (by what you see). [You condemn by external, human standards.] I do not [set Myself up to] judge or condemn or sentence anyone"* (AMPC). When the law condemned us, the Father and the Son came to rescue us all from the condemnation of the law.

I just find it amazing that after years of being a Christian, I never saw this. Somehow, through all the religious teaching and scriptures used to portray God as judging the world, I missed the very words of Jesus Christ Himself. Truth spoke in John 5:22, and He said, "The Father judges, condemns, and accuses no one." Truth spoke in John 5:45 and John 8:15, and He said,

"The Law is what condemns you, but I do not set Myself up to judge or condemn or sentence anyone!"

Truth spoke and revealed the true heart of the Father, and I have chosen to believe Him. I'm so happy to know the true character of my Good, Good Father, and no religious teaching will ever be able to deceive me into believing He judges, condemns, or punishes anyone ever again! He is the same yesterday, today, and forever! I have seen the Truth in the face of Jesus, and the Truth has set me free!

Jesus Revealed the Father's Heart Toward Those Who Don't Believe

Luke 9:53-56:

> "53But [the people] would not welcome or receive or accept Him. 54And when His disciples James and John observed this, they said, Lord, do You wish us to command fire to come down from heaven and consume them, even as Elijah did? 55But He turned and rebuked and severely censured them. He said, You do not know of what sort of spirit you are, 56For the Son of Man did not come to destroy men's lives, but to save them" (AMPC).

Jesus taught us so clearly in these verses that those who preach that the Father is judging or punishing people for their sins do not know the true heart of the Father. When the disciples wanted to judge those who did not accept Jesus, He rebuked them strongly and made the truth very clear to them when He said, "The Son of man did not come to destroy men's lives, but to save them!"

The Father did not send Jesus to condemn man. Romans 5:18 says that all men were trapped in condemnation. And Jesus came to rescue them. He didn't come to judge or punish them for their sin, but to offer them His free gift of eternal life!

Jesus Reveals the Father's Heart Toward Those Who Act Wickedly

Luke 6:35-36:

> *"35Love your enemies! Do good to them. Lend to them without expecting to be repaid. Then your reward from heaven will be very great, and you will truly be acting as children of the Most High, for he is kind and merciful to those who are unthankful and wicked"* (NLT).

> *"36Show mercy and compassion for others, just as your heavenly Father overflows with mercy and compassion for all"* (TPT).

Jesus said that when you love your enemies and do good to those who don't deserve it, you are acting just like your Father. Your Heavenly Father is not angry at the unthankful and wicked. Jesus said He is kind, compassionate and merciful to all!

Our Good Father Has Given Us the Ministry of Reconciliation

2 Corinthians 5:18-21:

> *"18And all of this is a gift from God, who brought us back to himself through Christ. And God has given us this task of reconciling people to him. 19For God was in Christ, reconciling the world to himself, no longer counting people's sins against them. And he gave us this wonderful message of reconciliation.*
>
> *20So we are Christ's ambassadors; God is making his appeal through us. We speak for Christ when we plead, "Come back to God!" 21For God made Christ, who never sinned, to be the offering for our sin, so that we could be made right with God through Christ"* (NLT).

Our Good Father has given us the ministry of reconciling people to Him. If you have never said, "Yes," to Jesus, I invite you right now to come back to God. Say, "Yes," to Jesus! He greatly loves and dearly prizes you. The Father is not judging nor condemning you. He sent Jesus to save you from the guilt and condemnation of the law by forgiving all your sins! He's not holding your sins against you.

You are His treasure. You are His pearl of great price. Jesus became sin so that you might be the righteousness of God in Him (2 Cor. 5:21). Just say, "Yes," to Jesus. Believe that He proved His great love for you by giving His life for you. Believe that He rose again to make you righteous, and you will experience everlasting life in the arms of Perfect Love!

REFLECTION AND DISCUSSION
QUESTIONS FOR CHAPTER 2

1. Have you ever been taught or believed that God is angry and judgmental toward those who sin? Have you heard preachers say that God is judging America? How did that make you feel about God?

2. There are many teachings about the character of God, but, according to Jesus, how will you find the truth about the character of the Father? (John 1:17-18).

3. 2 Corinthians 3:14-17 tells us that the veil of the law has blinded many people's minds, and they have lost the ability to understand the truth. How is the veil removed?

4. What did Jesus clearly teach us about the Father's heart toward the world in John 3:16-18?

5. Jesus said clearly in John 5:22 that "The Father judges no one!" Do you believe Him? If the Father is not judging or condemning the world, where did Jesus say the judgment is coming from? (John 5:45).

6. In John 8:3-11, what did Jesus reveal about the Father's heart toward those caught in sin? What did Jesus say in John 8:15 to the religious leaders of the day to correct the judgment that was in their heart toward those caught in sin?

7. In Luke 9:53-56, Jesus rebuked His disciples for even suggesting that He judge or condemn

people who did not believe or accept Him. How do you think He feels about people who are still claiming that God is judging America today? What did Jesus reveal about the Father's heart toward unbelievers in this story found in the Gospel of Luke?

8. In Luke 6:35-36, what did Jesus reveal about the Father's heart toward those who act wickedly? How can we act like our Father?

9. As Christ's ambassadors, what are we to tell the world about our Good Father? What is the ministry He has called us all to? (2 Corinthians 5:18-21).

Chapter 3
Living Free From the Religious Lie That There is Something Wrong with You

I have heard many messages over the course of my life that were focused on what I needed to do to be a better Christian: messages that made me feel that I wasn't quite good enough. They made me feel that I needed to pray more, give more, serve more, and love more.

I would attempt to do those things, but always seemed to fall short, and even though I wasn't aware of it, the lie of religion became deeply embedded in my heart: *There is something wrong with you and you need to fix it.* It's a condemning feeling that focuses on your weaknesses, your sins, and your failures.

Religion takes the focus off what Jesus did for us and places it on what we need to do for Him. When the focus is Jesus, it produces joy, peace, and love in our hearts. However, when the focus is placed on us, it produces pride, condemnation, guilt, fear, discouragement, and even depression. This lie—*There's something wrong with me*—is often disguised with these questions we ask ourselves:

- ❖ Why can't I lose weight?
- ❖ Why do I feel like a failure?
- ❖ Why do I feel so sad and discouraged?
- ❖ Why is it not working for me?
- ❖ Why are my prayers not being answered?
- ❖ Why do I struggle to believe God?
- ❖ Why do I worry so much about what people think?
- ❖ Why can't I stay focused to get this project done?

The list goes on and on, but the same question continually comes up in our hearts: *What's wrong with me?* Every time we look at our weaknesses, failures, or areas of our lives where we feel we don't measure up, the voice of condemnation continues to speak to our hearts and says, "There's something wrong with you!"

The interesting thing is that people often think it's only the religious system which causes them to feel like they're not good enough, yet the world's system does the very same thing. When we measure ourselves by the world's standards, we feel:

- ❖ I'm not thin enough.
- ❖ I'm not pretty enough.
- ❖ I'm not successful enough.
- ❖ I lack in some way.

The very root of condemnation is the belief that there is something wrong with you.

Where Did This Lie Come From?

It began in the Garden of Eden. After creating man and woman in Their image, the Father, Son, and Holy Spirit looked at them with eyes of Perfect Love. God said, "You are good—so very good—and I approve of you completely! You are excellent in every way!" (Genesis 1:27, 31).

That was the identity the Father had given mankind. We were created in His image (just like God)—perfect in every way. That's how the father defined us.

Then He said to Adam and Eve, "There's a tree in this garden, and I don't want you to eat from it. It is the tree of the knowledge of good and evil, of blessings and curses." The Father explained that if they chose to move outside of the identity that He had given them, trying to find their lives by defining themselves according to their own opinions (or the opinions of others), they would die. He was telling them that the condemning voice that they were not good enough would bring death to their souls.

Then Genesis 3:1-7 tells us that the enemy came and lied to them and said, "Can you really trust what God says about you? **You're not like God.** If you want to be like God, eat from the tree of the knowledge of good and evil, blessings and curses. Then you'll be wise and get to define yourselves. You'll be just like God. You'll get to judge what's good and what's bad." Adam and Eve believed the lie, and religion was born!

That tree represents the list of what you think you have to do to be like God—the list of what you have to do to be approved by God. It is the **do-do list** that tells your heart that you'll never be good enough!

Mankind began to live by the law that condemned them and told them over and over again, "There is something wrong with you." Once they ate from the tree that judged them good if they did good and bad if they did bad, they were trapped in condemnation because **they began to define themselves by their behavior,** which told them, "You're not good enough."

Genesis 3:7-11:

> *"7At that moment their eyes were opened, and they suddenly felt shame at their nakedness. So they sewed fig leaves together to cover themselves. 8When the cool evening breezes were blowing, the man and his wife heard the Lord God walking about in the garden. So they hid from the Lord God among the trees. 9Then the Lord God called to the man, "Where are you?" 10He replied, "I heard you walking in the garden, so I hid. I was afraid because I was naked." 11"Who told you that you were naked?"* (NLT).

The Father said, "Who told you that you were naked? Who told you there was something wrong with you? Did you eat from that which brings you death?" The moment they ate from that tree and got their identities from something other than their Father's good opinion of them, shame and fear entered their hearts, and they immediately felt badly about themselves.

I ate from that same tree for many years of my life. I believed the lie of religion that told me I wasn't good enough; there was something wrong with me; I needed to have more faith, be more kind, pray more, give more, and serve more, if I wanted to be more like Jesus.

Constantly trying to find approval in what I did left my heart filled with fear and shame. Just like 2 Corinthians 3:6 tells us, the law was condemning me. Yet, the Spirit came to give me life!

Our Good Father had a plan from the beginning of time to redeem and rescue us from the condemnation of the law of sin and death! Our wrong behavior told us that we weren't good enough, that something was wrong with us, but our Good Father never wanted us to be defined by our behavior. He wants us to find our identities in His Perfect Love—His never-changing good opinion of us in Christ!

The Truth That Set Me Free!

Ephesians 1:4:

> *"Even before he made the world, God loved us and chose us in Christ to be holy and without fault in his eyes"* (NLT).

Colossians 1:13-14, 22-23:

> *"13For he has rescued us from the kingdom of darkness and transferred us*

> into the Kingdom of his dear Son, **14**who
> purchased our freedom and forgave our
> sins... **22**now he has reconciled you to
> himself through the death of Christ in his
> physical body. As a result, he has
> brought you into his own presence, and
> you are holy and blameless as you stand
> before him without a single fault.
>
> **23But you must continue to believe
> this truth** and stand firmly in it. Don't
> drift away from the assurance you
> received when you heard the Good
> News" (NLT, emphasis mine).

The Gospel is Good News! The Good News is that you've been reconciled to God through the death of Jesus Christ, and you stand holy, blameless, and without a single fault in His sight. But you must believe this truth and stand in it firmly!

Don't ever let a religious lie, or a religious teaching, tell you that there's something wrong with you, when the Scriptures are so clear that, in Christ Jesus, you are without fault, forgiven, holy and blameless in your Father's eyes! When you embrace this truth, your whole life changes.

I know mine has. The voices of condemnation still try to come at me, but I now know the Truth, and the Truth has set me free! Jesus made me holy, righteous, and perfect in His sight, and His good opinion of us in Christ never changes.

The identity that He gave us is not based on our behavior. We still fail at times, but that doesn't change who we are. Our Good Father sent Jesus to rescue us from that lying, condemning thought that there's something wrong with us.

So, What is the Answer to the Question, "What is Wrong with Me?"

The answer to that question is found in the words of truth. Jesus is the Truth, and He spoke to you in Song of Songs 4:7:

> *"Everything about you is beautiful, and there is nothing AT ALL wrong with you!"* (NCV, emphasis mine).

That's what Jesus says about you. The question is, will you believe Him?

When you said, "Yes," to Jesus, you became the Bride of Christ. Jesus, your Husband, has spoken to your heart and said that everything about you is beautiful, and there is nothing at all wrong with you! Jesus is the Truth about you!

Isn't that the best news you have ever heard?

Recently, I had someone tell me that someone said, "I don't believe what Connie teaches about 'There is nothing wrong with us.'"

I replied, "Isn't that interesting, because I am not the one who said it: Jesus is. If a person doesn't believe that there is nothing at all wrong with them, it's not me they don't believe. They don't believe Jesus."

If Song of Songs 4:7 doesn't persuade your heart of this truth, listen to what Ephesians 5:26-27 says:

> *"26Christ used the word to make the church clean by washing it with water. 27He died so that he could give the church to himself like a bride in all her beauty. He died so that the church could be pure and without fault, with no evil or sin or any other wrong thing in it"* (NCV).

Jesus cleanses our hearts from the condemning voice that tells us there's something wrong with us by reminding us that we are His beautiful bride, pure and without fault in His sight. Because we are one with Him, He says there is no sin or any other wrong thing in us. There is nothing at all wrong with us!

What if every time that accusing voice of condemnation came up in your heart, you responded with the truth, "There's nothing wrong with me!" How would it change the course of your life? This lie is so deeply embedded in our hearts that sometimes we don't even know it's there. This view of ourselves keeps us in the vicious cycle of condemnation and failure.

Recently, a friend, who struggles with her weight, said to me, "Connie, since you started teaching this truth, I realize that's the lie I've always believed about myself. 'I can't lose weight! What's wrong with me?'"

I also had a friend who struggles with addictions say the same thing. As I listened to them talk, I realized the simplicity of why people struggle in so many areas of their life, never seeming to experience the freedom that Jesus paid such a great price for us to live in!

We have been deceived by this lie that something is wrong with us! It's so subtle that sometimes you don't even recognize it. But if there is an area of your life in which you have been disappointed with yourself, I can guarantee this lie is lurking deep within your heart.

It's Time for Freedom!

It's time that the very root of condemnation be uprooted and completely eliminated from your heart! It reminds me of the movie, *Terminator*! The Terminator came back to destroy what was killing mankind. That's what Jesus did! Condemnation was killing mankind, and Jesus came and *terminated* condemnation by nailing every accusation against you to the cross!

Colossians 2:14-15:

> *"14He canceled out every legal violation we had on our record and the old arrest warrant that stood to indict us. He erased it all—our sins, our stained soul— he deleted it all and they cannot be retrieved! Everything we once were in Adam has been placed onto his cross and nailed permanently there as a public display of cancellation. 15Then Jesus made a public spectacle of all the powers and principalities of darkness, stripping away from them every weapon and all their spiritual authority and power to accuse us. And by the power of the cross, Jesus led them around as prisoners in a*

> *procession of triumph. He was not their
> prisoner; they were his!"* (TPT).

Romans 8:1-2:

> *"¹So now the case is closed. There
> remains no accusing voice of
> condemnation against those who are
> joined in life-union with Jesus"* (TPT).

> *"²because through Christ Jesus the law
> of the Spirit who gives life has set you
> free from the law of sin and death"* (NIV).

Jesus shut the mouth of every condemning, accusing voice by making you perfect forever by His one and final sacrifice. Through that sacrifice, He silenced any voice that causes condemnation.

Hebrews 10:14 says, *"For by that one offering he forever made perfect those who are being made holy"* (NLT).

Now you are free to live from your **true identity** in Christ! What you believe in your heart is what you'll experience in your life. If you believe the lie that something is wrong with you, you will continue to live under the condemnation of your own heart, and failure is what you'll experience. But if you'll lay that lie down and begin to embrace the truth that Jesus speaks over you, your life will bear much abundant fruit by the power of God's Spirit in you! (Galatians 5:22-23).

So, the next time you look at yourself—and you hear that accusing voice of condemnation trying to get you to ask the question, "What's wrong with me?"—respond to it just like Jesus did. Answer back with the truth: ***"It is written, Truth has spoken, and there is nothing at all wrong with me! Condemnation, you have been terminated!"***

REFLECTION AND DISCUSSION
QUESTIONS FOR CHAPTER 3

1. Have you ever heard a message that left you feeling like you weren't quite good enough? Have you ever believed the lie that there is something wrong with you, and you need to fix it? Share a negative thought you've had about yourself that reinforced the lie, "There's something wrong with you!"

2. Where did this lie come from? (Genesis 3:1-11) What negative emotions does this lie produce in our hearts?

3. According to Colossians 1:13-14; 22-23, what is the Good News that your Good Father wants you to believe about yourself? What is the truth that sets you free from this lie of religion?

4. What did Jesus say about you in Song of Songs 4:7? What is your initial thought when you hear your Savior say these words to you? Do you believe Him?

5. How does Jesus cleanse your heart from the condemning, accusing voice that tells you that there is something wrong with you? Why did He die for you? (Ephesians 5:26-27).

6. What does Colossians 2:13-14 tell you Jesus did with all your sins and any accusation that could ever tell you that there is something wrong with you?

7. In Romans 8:1-2, what do the words, "the case is closed" mean to you?

8. What did Jesus' one and final sacrifice make you? (Hebrews 10:14). How does that make your heart feel?

9. Now that you know the truth, will you let the devil continue to deceive you with the lie that there is something wrong with you? It's time for freedom!

Chapter 4
Religion Makes Fearful Slaves!
Jesus Made Fearless Sons!

Religion produced fear in my heart for many years of my life. I heard so many messages that focused on my behavior, and what I needed to do to earn God's favor and blessing. These messages held me captive to the fear of never quite being good enough.

Religion focuses on what man needs to do and creates fearful slaves, but the true Gospel focuses on what Jesus did and creates fearless sons. Religion uses fear to try to control people's behavior, but Jesus came to bring peace to our hearts by making us beloved sons. Has religion ever taught you something that created fear in your heart? You can be very sure that if a message brings you fear, it's a lie!

Many things that religion teaches produce fear in the human heart:

❖ Fear of hell.

❖ Fear of punishment.

❖ Fear of the end times.

❖ Fear of judgment. .

❖ Fear of being left behind.

❖ Fear of disapproval.

❖ Fear of never being good enough.

❖ Fear of things not working out well for you if you don't do everything right.

❖ Fear of what others think of you.

❖ Fear of being rejected if you don't follow all the rules.

❖ Fear, Fear and more Fear.

As a little girl, one of the fears that religion produced in my heart was the fear that Jesus might come back and leave me behind. I remember being at the grocery store with my mom; I couldn't find her anywhere, and fear gripped my heart. I thought surely Jesus had come back and left me behind!

That fear was created by a message I had heard in church about my behavior. I was taught that if I had unconfessed sin in my life then I would be left behind.

This same fear happened to my oldest son. When he was about 11 years old, he was spending the night at a friend's house. He woke up in the middle of the night and couldn't find his brother or his friend. So, he sat on the couch and cried because he thought Jesus had come back and left him behind. I never taught my son that! That fear was put into his heart by a message he heard at church. Religion told him that if he wasn't good enough, he might be left behind.

I remember how upset I was when I found out that he had been taught the same lie that I had believed when I was his age. When he came home that day and told me about what had happened, I said, "Justin, Jesus loves you and He promised you in Hebrews 13:5 that He would never leave you nor forsake you. Don't ever believe anyone who teaches you that Jesus might leave you behind, because that is a lie."

When I shared that truth with him, he was set free from that fear, and peace came to his heart. The true Gospel is the Gospel of Peace. When you hear it, it never produces fear. It always produces the fruit of peace. If a message you hear brings fear to your heart, you can be absolutely sure that it is a lie!

Religion Uses Fear—Jesus' Perfect Love Drives Fear Away

Religion uses fear to control people's behavior, but Jesus' Perfect Love drives fear far from our hearts!

1 John 4:16,18:

> *"16We have come into an intimate experience with God's love, and we trust in the love he has for us. God is love!...*

> **18*Love never brings fear***, *for fear is always related to punishment. But love's perfection drives the fear of punishment far from our hearts..."* (TPT, emphasis mine).

These verses make it very clear that God is Love. Verse 18 tells us that the Father, the Son, and the Holy Spirit never bring fear. Love's perfection drives the fear of punishment far from our hearts. So, if anyone delivers a message that produces fear in our hearts, we can know that it did not come from God. **Perfect Love casts out all fear**! When you believe what the Father, the Son, and the Holy Spirit teach you, you live fearless and enjoy great peace!

Perfect Love Brings Perfect Peace

In John 14:27, Jesus said, *"I am leaving you with a gift—peace of mind and heart. And the peace I give is a gift the world cannot give. So don't be troubled or afraid"* (NLT).

In John 16:33, Jesus said, *"I have told you these things, so that in Me **you may have [perfect] peace and confidence**"* (AMPC, emphasis mine).

Everything Jesus speaks to our hearts produces perfect peace and confidence. He said He left us with the gift of peace of mind and heart. So, if a message you hear does not produce perfect peace and confidence in your heart, it's not the truth! It's not the true Gospel, and it didn't come from Jesus, because He is the Prince of Peace.

If you believe what Jesus said, you'll never be deceived by religion another day in your life. You'll be able to discern whether a message you hear is the truth or a lie. Do not accept any message that brings fear. Listen to your heart. You are led by God's Spirit. You hear God's voice and His voice always brings peace. It always brings confidence. It always makes you feel alive. It never brings condemnation, and it never brings fear. If it's not producing joy and peace to your heart, it's not the Gospel! Period!

Take Away the Fear, and the Controlling Religious System Comes Tumbling Down!

The very purpose of fear is to control! I love this statement made by my good friend and fellow minister of grace, Pieter Swart: "If I preach a message that establishes your heart in fear—I can control you. The Gospel always establishes the heart in grace and peace. A heart filled with peace cannot be controlled. It is wide open for the guidance of the Spirit."

Let's just think about that. Take away the fear of hell. Take away the fear of disapproval or punishment. Take away the fear of the end-times or being left behind. Take away the fear of never being good enough. Take away the fear of judgment. Take away the fear of rejection and what other people think of you. You take away the fear, and the whole controlling religious system comes tumbling down!

No one can control you anymore when you know who you are in Jesus. You're a beloved child of God. You are blessed, righteous, and approved because of Jesus! You are no longer striving to become, because you know you already are! All the promise of God are

Yes and Amen in your life, so you don't need any more sermons telling you how to qualify for them. WOOHOO! FREEDOM!!

This truth has changed my life! The belief that I'm not a fearful slave trying to earn God's promises, but that I am a beloved child who is an heir of the promises of God, has brought such peace and rest in my life.

For example, I can't even count how many messages I had heard on how to hear God's voice. There was always something I needed to *do* to hear God better. I was constantly trying to hear His voice and wasn't quite sure I would hear it. But when I discovered the truth in John 10:5, where Jesus said that I hear His voice and the voice of a stranger I don't follow, I simply began to believe what was true about me. I no longer needed twenty messages on how to hear God's voice, because it is simply who I am.

When you are no longer focused on what you need to do, but rather simply embracing who you are in Jesus, you begin to experience the peace of heart and mind that Jesus promised. When you believe that you hear God's voice and you follow it, you'll no longer be afraid of not hearing Him.

I remember how my thoughts changed from worry and concern in this area to simply praying, "Father, I thank you that I hear your voice, and I follow your voice. You are causing my thoughts to be agreeable to your will, and my plans are established and succeed" (Proverbs 16:3).

When your focus changes from you to Jesus, you begin to live from a place of confidence and peace.

Romans 8:14 tells us that the sons of God are led by His Spirit. That's what's true about me, and that's what's true about you. All we have to do is simply believe it!

Religion Makes Fearful Slaves—Jesus Made us Fearless Sons!

❖ Slaves are controlled by outward rules and fear of the consequences if they don't follow them.

❖ Sons are led by God's Spirit: they live from who they are in Christ—beloved children of God.

Romans 8:14-15:

> *"14For as many as are led by the Spirit of God, these are sons of God"* (NKJV).

> *"15So you have not received a spirit that makes you **fearful slaves**. Instead, you received God's Spirit when he adopted you as his own children. Now we call him, 'Abba, Father'"* (NLT, emphasis mine).

Romans 8:15-17:

> *"15You did not receive the **"spirit of religious duty,"** leading you back into the fear of never being good enough**. But you have received the **"Spirit of full acceptance,"** enfolding you into the family of God. And you will never feel orphaned, for as he rises up within us, our spirits join him in saying*

> *the words of tender affection, "Beloved*
> *Father!"* *16For the Holy Spirit makes*
> *God's fatherhood real to us as he*
> *whispers into our innermost being,*
> ***"You are God's beloved child!"***
>
> *17And since we are his true children, **we***
> ***qualify** to share all his treasures, for*
> *indeed, we are heirs of God himself. And*
> *since we are joined to Christ, we also*
> *inherit all that he is and all that he has"*
> (TPT, emphasis mine).

That is the best news I have ever heard! We qualify to share in all His treasures simply because we are His beloved children. You are not fearful slaves trying to qualify yourselves. You never have to fear not being good enough. You are fully accepted. You have a Father who dearly loves you. You qualify for all of His promises. You are an heir of God. You inherit all that He is and all that He has, simply because you are His beloved child. You are a joint heir with Jesus.

All you need to do is simply embrace your true identity. Never let a message you hear take your focus off of Jesus and who you are in Him. It's not about what you need to do, but rather what Jesus did for you. You never have to be afraid of Him, or afraid you don't qualify. You are favored! You are righteous! You hear God's voice! And every detail of your life is being worked into something good! You are blessed because of Jesus! That's the true Good News of the Gospel!

Whenever I feel afraid, as we all do at times, I turn my heart and thoughts to my Good, Good Father. For I know He will never be angry with me, never judge me, never leave me nor forsake me, or change His good opinion of me. His Perfect Love casts out all my fear! Like a little child who feels loved by their daddy, I run to my daddy who I know will take care of me, love me, and protect me—not because I've done everything right, but just because I am His!

Everything He is and everything He has is mine. I am an heir to all His promises because I am His beloved child. His perfect Love fills my heart with perfect peace.

What About the Fear of the Lord?

The Bible is full of verses regarding the fear of the Lord. In order to rightly divide the Word of Truth, we must know what the word "fear" in these verses really means. The Hebrew and Greek words for "fear" mean "reverent or reverence" (Strong's H3373; Strong's G5401).

The word reverence means deep respect for someone or something. Synonyms of reverence are esteem, respect, admiration, and adoration (dictionary .com/browse/reverence).

So, when you "Fear the Lord," it doesn't mean you are afraid of Him, but rather that you hold Him in high esteem, great respect and admiration. When you walk in the fear of the Lord, you're not afraid of God. You believe Him. A person who fears the Lord believes Him when He says, "You are loved. You are blessed. You are favored and righteous in My sight!"

People who fear the Lord will hold what God says about them in such high esteem that they will let go of their opinions of themselves and others, and they will believe what God says, because they greatly respect Him.

So, let's rightly divide the Word of God. We don't fear God by being afraid of His punishment. We fear God by respecting, honoring and appreciating Him by believing what He says about us. When you believe what He says about you, you are walking in the fear of the Lord—you highly respect and esteem Him and appreciate everything He's done for you in Christ.

As a Beloved Child of God, You Are an Heir of His Promises

Galatians 4:4-10, 12, 28:

> "*4But when that era came to an end and the time of fulfillment had come, God sent his Son, born of a woman, born under the written law. 5Yet all of this was so that **he would redeem and set free all those held hostage to the written law** so that we would receive our freedom and a full legal adoption as his children.*
>
> *6And so that we would know for sure that we are his true children, God released the Spirit of Sonship into our hearts—moving us to cry out intimately, "My Father! You're our true Father!"*
>
> *7**Now we're no longer living like slaves under the law, but we enjoy***

being God's very own sons and daughters! *And because we're his, we can access everything our Father has— for we are heirs of God through Jesus, the Messiah!*

⁸Before we knew God as our Father and we became his children, we were unwitting servants to the powers that be, which are nothing compared to God. **⁹But now that we truly know him and understand how deeply we're loved by him, why would we, even for a moment, consider turning back to those weak and feeble principles of religion, as though we were still subject to them?**

¹⁰Why would we want to go backwards into the bondage of religion...?" (TPT, emphasis mine).

"¹²Beloved ones, I plead with you, follow my example and become free from the bondage of religion" (TPT).

"²⁸Dear friends, just like Isaac, we're now the true children who inherit the kingdom promises" (TPT).

These verses make it so clear that we are no longer living like slaves under the law of written rules, trying to keep all the commands so we can stand righteous before God. I can't even say it any clearer than the verses we just read. We are not fearful slaves, but rather we enjoy being God's very own sons and daughters—heirs of all His promises. Because we are His, we can access everything our Father has, for we are heirs of God through Jesus.

Verse 8 says that before we understood who we are, we were unwitting servants to the powers that be. The word "unwitting" means to not be aware of the full truth: to be in the dark (www.dictionary.com/browse /unwitting).

We were in the dark before we understood how much God loved us. We were not aware of the full truth that Jesus made us righteous and good. Therefore, we were subject to be deceived with the lie that we weren't good enough. We were deceived by the lies of religion.

But now that we know who we are, no one can deceive us into believing we have to do something to qualify for our Father's blessing. Now that we truly know Him and understand how deeply we're loved by Him, why would we even consider for a moment turning back to those weak and feeble rules of religion?

Why would we ever want to go back to trying to live by a bunch of religious rules when we have the Spirit of God in us, reminding us who we are and empowering us to bear the fruit of righteousness? We live and move and have our being in Jesus (Acts 17:28).

Galatians 5:22-23 tells us that the Spirit of God within us produces this kind of fruit in our lives: love, joy, peace, goodness, kindness, gentleness, humility, faithfulness and self-control—against such there is no law! You don't need a law to live by when you have the Spirit of God living on the inside of you telling you who you are. When you believe you're righteous in Jesus, the Spirit of God produces righteous fruit in your life.

The greatest life you'll ever find is found in believing who you are in Jesus. When you embrace your true identity, you will love yourself and others effortlessly! That's the fruit of the true Gospel of Jesus Christ.

Galatians 3:18 says, *"We receive all the promises because of the Promised One—not because we keep the law!"* (TPT).

WOW! This verse is so clear! It says we receive all the promises because of the Promised One, not because we keep the law. Don't ever believe the lie of religion that you receive the promises by obeying the law, when the Scriptures teach quite the opposite.

2 Corinthians 1:20:

> *"The yes to all of God's promises is in Christ, and through Christ we say yes to the glory of God"* (NCV).

The yes to all of God's promises is in Christ. It's not in your performance. It's not in you keeping the law perfectly. It's not in you trying to qualify yourself. The yes to all of God's promises are in Christ Jesus. That means that if you are in Christ, then your Good Father has already said, "Yes!" to all His promises to you. You can rest in His great love.

You don't need to listen to another message telling you how to qualify for God's promises. You're already qualified. The answer is already, "Yes." Now you get to decide if you will say, "Yes," to Jesus. You get to decide:

Am I going to live my life as a fearful slave trying to earn God's promises or am I simply going to live like a beloved child and say, "Father, I say 'Yes' to my true identity in Jesus! I am who you say I am! Because what you say about me is true!"

That's how you live like a fearless son: by saying yes to all of God's promises. When you are facing a negative situation, you can either look to yourself and live as a fearful slave or look to Jesus and live as a fearless son.

There's a better way to live! When we truly embrace that we are beloved children, who are led by God's Spirit and heirs of His promises, we will experience the perfect peace that Jesus came to give us all! We will finally live free from the fear and control of religion and truly enjoy our lives as beloved children who are blessed because of Jesus!

REFLECTION AND DISCUSSION
QUESTIONS FOR CHAPTER 4

1. Have you ever been taught something in church that brought fear to your heart? Recall some of those teachings.

2. Religion uses fear to control people's behavior. How can you know that any teaching that produces fear does not come from God? What does His perfect Love do? Discuss 1 John 4:16,18.

3. What does the truth produce in your heart? What did Jesus promise in John 14:27 and John 16:33?

4. Can religious teaching control you with fear if you know the truth of God's Love? Why?

5. What's the difference between living as a fearful slave and living as a fearless son? (Romans 8:14-17)

6. What does it mean to fear the Lord?

7. Now that you know how deeply you are loved, why would you ever want to go back to the bondage of religion? Discuss the truth found in Galatians 4:4-10, 12, 28.

8. Why are you an heir to all of God's promises? Is it because of what you have done or because of what Jesus has done for you? (Galatians 3:18 and 2 Corinthians 1:20).

Chapter 5
The Lie Religion Taught Me
About Tithing

The lie that religion has taught in the church today is that tithing qualifies us for God's blessing. It is often taught that if you don't tithe, you'll be cursed. I've even heard messages in church that said if you don't give God His ten percent, He will get it from you in some way.

This message produces fear in the hearts of those who hear it. It causes people to tithe and give based on fear instead of love. Let's read 1 John 4:16,18 again, because if you understand this one passage of Scripture, you'll never be deceived by a message that produces fear in your heart ever again.

1 John 4:16 and 18 says, "*16...God is love...* *18Love NEVER brings fear, for fear is always related to*

punishment. But love's perfection drives the fear of punishment far from our hearts..." (TPT, emphasis mine).

This scripture is so clear. God is love! The Father, the Son and the Holy Spirit will never bring fear to our hearts. Fear is related to punishment. But God's Perfect Love for us drives the fear of punishment far from our hearts. The true Gospel never brings fear, but rather drives fear away. If what you believe about God produces fear in your heart, you can be sure it is a lie!

Where Did This Lie Come From?

Malachi 3:8-10:

> "8Will a man rob God? Yet you have robbed Me! But you say, 'In what way have we robbed You?' In tithes and offerings. 9You are cursed with a curse, For you have robbed Me, Even this whole nation. 10Bring all the tithes into the storehouse, That there may be food in My house, And try Me now in this," Says the Lord of hosts, "If I will not open for you the windows of heaven And pour out for you such blessing That there will not be room enough to receive it" (NKJV).

That sounds pretty convincing, doesn't it? This passage of Scripture had convinced me that what religion taught must be true, and it brought fear to my heart for many years. I heard so many messages from

Malachi 3:8-10 that told me that I could earn God's blessing by tithing, but if I didn't tithe, I would be under God's curse.

Oh, the bondage of pride that came into my heart when I kept that law, and oh, the bondage of fear if I didn't! I believed this lie for far too many years!

The Truth That Set Me Free!

My eyes were opened through Galatians 3:10-14, 18:

> "*¹⁰All who depend on the Law [who are seeking to be justified by obedience to the Law] are under a curse and **doomed to disappointment**"* (AMPC, emphasis mine).

> "*¹⁰But if you choose to live in bondage under the legalistic rule of religion, you live under the law's curse. For it is clearly written: "Utterly cursed is everyone who fails to practice every detail and requirement that is written in this Law!"*

> *¹¹For the Scriptures reveal, and it is obvious, that no one achieves the righteousness of God by attempting to keep the law, for it is written: "Those who have been made holy will live by faith!"*

> *¹²But keeping the law does not require faith, but self-effort. For the Law*

teaches, *"If you practice the principles of law, You must follow all of them."*

¹³Yet, **Jesus paid the full price to set us free from the curse of the law.** He absorbed it completely as he became a *"curse"* in our place. For it is written: *"Everyone who is hung upon a tree is doubly cursed."*

¹⁴Jesus, our Messiah was hung upon a *"tree,"* **bearing the curse in our place and in so doing, dissolved it from our lives,** so that all the blessings of Abraham can be poured out upon us! And now God shows grace to all of us and gives us the promise of the wonderful Holy Spirit who lives within us when we believe in him...

¹⁸We receive all the promises because of the Promised One—not because we keep the law!" (TPT, emphasis mine).

Wow! This passage of Scripture could not be any clearer. Galatians 3:10 says that under the New Covenant of grace, all who depend on obedience to the law to be blessed by God are under a curse and doomed to disappointed. No wonder I had become so disappointed!

I had actually believed that I could earn God's blessing by following the law of tithing, but verse 10 makes it very clear that if you or I choose to live in bondage under a legalistic rule of religion, we live under the law's curse. For it is clearly written: "Utterly

cursed is everyone who fails to practice **every detail
and requirement that is written in the Law.**"

The Scriptures actually say that if we are going to
depend on our obedience to the law to qualify us for
God's blessing, we must obey every detail of the law
perfectly. So, if we want to live by the law of tithing,
we must read every scripture on tithing and follow
every detail. Those details concerning tithing can be
found in:

- ❖ Leviticus 27:30-34

- ❖ Numbers 18:21-28

- ❖ Deuteronomy 12:6-17; 14:22-28; 26:1-13

- ❖ 2 Chronicles 31:5-12

- ❖ Nehemiah 10:37-38 and 12:44; 13:5-12

We all know that nobody can keep all the details of
the law perfectly. That's why what Jesus did for us is
such Good News! Galatians 3:13 says that Jesus paid
the *full price* to set us free from the curse of the law. He
dissolved the curse from our lives, so that the blessing
of Abraham can be poured upon us through faith in
Him! Galatians 3:18 clearly reveals that we receive
God's promises because of Jesus, not because we keep
the law.

Like so many believers today, I lived for years under
the religious lie that my actions would somehow earn
God's blessing in my life. Ever since the day we were
married, my husband and I made sure we tithed on
every dime because we wanted God's blessing and we
sure didn't want to be cursed!

After many years of tithing, we continued to struggle in our finances and often came up short. We actually found ourselves putting our basic needs on credit cards to make ends meet. We heard all those testimonies of people who began tithing and were blessed by God, but there was never any mention of Jesus in those testimonies. They were testifying of what they did to qualify for God's blessing. They never mentioned what *Jesus* did to qualify *them*. This only pointed us to ourselves and caused us to question, "What are we doing wrong? We must not be giving enough."

Then, one Christmas we were given $1000 by a family member. I remember thinking, *Maybe if we give this away, we will get our breakthrough.* I heard a preacher on TV say if we gave $1,000 to his ministry we would get a hundredfold return. Again, there was no mention of what Jesus did for us, only what we needed to do to qualify for God's blessing.

So, we gave our thousand dollars away, but still nothing changed! We were so disappointed. Galatians 3:10 had proven true in our lives. We had depended on our obedience to earn God's blessing, and we were doomed to disappointment.

I remember the turning point in my life, when I realized I was no longer bound underneath this religious lie. I went to talk to my sister about how disappointed I had become. I poured my heart out to her, explaining how we had been tithing and giving for years, and we were still struggling to make ends meet. I expected her to tell me one more thing that I needed to do to qualify, but instead she said something that changed my life forever.

She looked at me and said, "Connie, I don't know what to tell you, because it's not working for me either." She was living in disappointment too, and I didn't even know it! When my sister, who I respected, who had graduated from Bible School, who seemed to follow all the rules, said those words to me, I thought, *We have been duped! Something is not right! I bet it's not working for a whole lot of people.*

I went home that day, and I cried out to Jesus. I said, "Lord, I've been tithing and giving for years. I've read all these books on what to do to be financially blessed by You, and it's not working for me. I feel so disappointed. Show me the truth that will set me free!"

That day, the Spirit of God took me to Galatians 3:10-18. As I read those verses, the eyes of my understanding were opened. The Lord showed me through those scriptures that I had been trusting in what I did to qualify for His blessing, instead of trusting in what Jesus did for me! I realized I had been trying to live by the Old Testament Law of Malachi 3:8-10, thinking it was up to me to earn God's blessing and save myself from the curse. I hadn't been living in the freedom of the New Covenant found in Galatians 3:10-18, in which Jesus paid the full price to set me free from the curse of the law and qualify me for all of God's blessings!

Galatians 3:18 solidified this truth in my heart. Let's read it again:

> *"18We receive all the promises because of the Promised One—not because we keep the law!"* (TPT).

The day I saw this truth, I jumped up out of my chair, began dancing a happy dance in the circle of God's love, and I've been dancing there ever since! I began to shout, "I'm blessed because of Jesus! It's because of You, Jesus, that I am blessed!"

It was the day of freedom for me. I just kept repeating those words, over and over again—rejoicing in what Jesus had done for me—until the truth so deeply penetrated my heart that it completely uprooted the lies I had believed.

This religious lie I had believed was not going to hold me in bondage another day in my life. No more fear! No more condemnation! No more disappointment! I was finally free! Free to believe that I am blessed because of Jesus! Free to give from a heart filled with His love!

The law of tithing caused me to give out of obligation and fear, but the truth set me free to give with a joyful heart of love. **I love to give!** It is the joy of my heart to give to those in need and to support my church. It is the joy of my heart to give to ministries that are preaching the Good News of the Gospel of Jesus. **The law never produced that joy in me,** but the fruit of the Spirit came forth when I simply believed that I am blessed to be a blessing because of Jesus!

What About Abraham? Didn't He Tithe Before the Law?

Sometimes people use the story of Abraham to try to convince others that tithing was before the law, so they should still feel obligated to tithe. But the truth is that **Abraham didn't tithe to be blessed.** Genesis 14:18-20 tells us that Abraham was blessed first by Melchizedek, king of Salem, who was a type and shadow of Jesus. He tithed after God had already abundantly blessed him. Abraham did not follow any law to be blessed. He tithed because that was in his heart to do.

If it's in your heart to give 10% of all that God has blessed you with, then give it joyfully, but don't give it to qualify yourself—you're already qualified because of Jesus. God spoke to Abraham in Genesis 12:2-3, before he ever tithed, and said, **"I will bless you and you will be a blessing."** And He is speaking that same promise to us all, because of Jesus!

Is Tithing Mentioned in the New Testament?

If we are required to tithe, don't you think it would have been taught in the New Testament? There are only three places where tithing is even mentioned in the Gospels.

The first two are in Matthew 23:23 and Luke 11:42. In these verses, Jesus was talking to the religious leaders of the day about the motivation of their hearts. He addressed the fact that they were tithing, and following a list of outward religious rules, but they didn't have love in their hearts.

These accounts were not Jesus teaching a New Covenant believer to tithe, but rather Jesus correcting man's wrong belief that it is their good works that justifies them. He was pointing out that they were trusting in what they did, and it was not producing love in their hearts.

2 Corinthians 13:3 further confirms this truth. It says that we can give everything we have away, but if it isn't motivated by love, it profits us nothing. Love is the fruit of the true Gospel. When you trust in God's love for you, love will be the fruit of your life. If what we believe is not producing love in our hearts, we are believing a lie!

People can list all their religious laws and rules about tithing, but the law never produces love in the hearts of those who hear it. It produces pride in those who think they are better than others because they tithe, and it produces fear and condemnation in those who think they are not good enough because they haven't.

I remember the day I heard the sweet sound of correction as Jesus took me to the third place tithing is mentioned in the Gospels and revealed the truth that would forever change my life.

In Luke 18:9-15, Jesus taught about men who trust in themselves and what they have done, instead of trusting in Jesus and what He has done for them:

> *"9Also He spoke this parable to some who trusted in themselves that they were righteous, and despised others: 10"Two men went up to the temple to pray, one a Pharisee and the other a tax collector. 11The Pharisee stood and prayed thus with himself, 'God, I thank You that I am not like other men—extortioners, unjust,*

adulterers, or even as this tax collector.
*¹²I fast twice a week; **I give tithes of***
all that I possess. *¹³And the tax*
collector, standing afar off, would not so
much as raise his eyes to heaven, but
beat his breast, saying, 'God, be merciful
to me a sinner!' ¹⁴I tell you, this man
went down to his house justified rather
than the other; for everyone who exalts
himself will be humbled, and he who
humbles himself will be exalted" (NKJV,
emphasis mine).

As I read this parable, I saw myself in that Pharisee.
I recalled how many times I had thought, *I'm tithing*
and giving. I'm not like those who don't tithe. I deserve
God's blessing. I had even at times told God how I was
obeying Him and because of that I was expecting His
blessing on my life.

That day, I saw the pride in my own heart. I had to
ask myself, *Who am I really trusting in? Myself, or*
Jesus? Was I trusting in my good works, or was I
trusting in His finished work?

The answer was clear: I expected God to bless me
because I tithed, not because of Jesus. I repented that
day, turned from that way of thinking and began to
trust Jesus as the only One who qualified me for God's
blessing upon my life.

The Lord corrected the way I believed that day, and
it was the sweet sound of correction. There was no
condemnation in it. It was the sound of freedom. My
Father wanted to free me from the lie that it was my
good works that qualified me so that I could experience
the fruit of believing that it's all because of Jesus!

When I took my eyes off myself and put my eyes on Jesus, my heart overflowed with thanksgiving. I remember thinking, *You really love us, Jesus! You really did free us from the curse so that we can experience your overflowing blessing upon our lives!*

When I put my trust in Jesus, it felt like the windows of heaven opened up. I not only began to experience so much love, joy, and peace in my heart, but also the abundant provision of Jesus in our lives. We were blessed in ways we couldn't even have imagined! Just like Abraham, we were able to give out of our abundance with thankful hearts. We were blessed to be a blessing because of Jesus!

Hebrews Chapter 7 is the Only Other Place Tithing is Mentioned in the New Testament.

This chapter of the Bible mentions tithing, but it's not for the purpose of teaching a New Covenant believer to tithe, but rather to teach us the difference between the Old Covenant Levitical priesthood, and Jesus. The Levitical priesthood was based on obedience to the law and required a continual sacrifice for the people's sins, but Jesus became our High Priest forever.

Hebrews 10:14 says that Jesus made us perfect forever and qualified us for God's blessing by His **one and final sacrifice**. The Old Covenant focused on man's performance and his good works, but the New Covenant focuses on Jesus and His finished work! The first covenant depended on your faithfulness to God, but the New Covenant depends on Jesus' faithfulness to you.

Hebrews 7:22 says, *"Jesus has become our Guarantee of a better agreement—a more excellent and more advantageous covenant"* (AMPC).

Hebrews 8:6 says, *"But now Jesus, our High Priest, has been given a ministry that is far superior to the old priesthood, for he is the one who mediates for us a far better covenant with God, based on better promises"* (NLT).

And Hebrews 8:13 says, *"When God speaks of a new [covenant or agreement], He makes the first one obsolete (out of use). And what is obsolete (out of use and annulled because of age) is ripe for disappearance and to be dispensed with altogether"* (AMPC).

A New Covenant! A New Way to Give! You Are Led by God's Spirit!

2 Corinthians 9:7-11:

> *"7Let giving flow from your heart, not from a sense of religious duty. Let it spring up freely from the joy of giving— all because God loves hilarious generosity!"* (TPT).

> *"8And God is able to make all grace (every favor and earthly blessing) come to you in abundance, so that you may always and under all circumstances and whatever the need be self-sufficient [possessing enough to require no aid or support and furnished in abundance for*

> *every good work and charitable
> donation]. ⁹As it is written, He [the
> benevolent person] scatters abroad; He
> gives to the poor; His deeds of justice
> and goodness and benevolence will go
> on and endure forever! ¹⁰And [God] Who
> provides seed for the sower and bread
> for eating will also provide and multiply
> your [resources for] sowing and
> increase the fruits of your righteousness
> [which manifests itself in active
> goodness, kindness, and charity]"*
> (AMPC).

> *"¹¹You will be enriched in every way so
> that you can be generous on every
> occasion, and through us your
> generosity will result in thanksgiving to
> God"* (NIV).

Grace is unmerited favor. It cannot be earned. Verse 8 tells us that all **grace** abounds toward you in abundance so that you can be generous on every occasion. The teaching that you must tithe to earn God's blessing contradicts this very verse.

Grace does not come to those who try to earn God's blessing, but rather to those who are humble enough to receive it. Pride says, "It's because of my giving that I'm blessed." Humility says, "I'm blessed because of Jesus!"

I remember the day this verse came alive in me! I simply began to thank my Good Father for causing all grace to abound toward me because of Jesus!

As New Covenant believers, we no longer live by the law. We live by the Spirit. We give generously, not in order to be blessed, but because we are blessed in Jesus. Jesus has given us loving, generous hearts, just like His!

We no longer have to submit to the control of religion telling us how much to give and where to give it. We are no longer controlled by fear and giving from a sense of religious duty, but we are free to give from hearts of love. We give to those in need and to every good work with joyful hearts. We are blessed to be a blessing because of Jesus! We are no longer fearful slaves to the law. We are beloved children of God! He takes care of us because He loves us, and we are His!

The Truth about Sowing and Reaping

Religious teaching has tried to convince us that we must sow to reap, but 2 Corinthians 9:10 clearly teaches that God provides us with seed to sow and bread to eat! Even beyond that, it says He will also multiply our resources for sowing. He will provide **more** than we need so we can be generous on every occasion!

In Matthew 6:26, Jesus said, *"Look at the birds of the air; they do not sow or reap or store away in barns, and yet your heavenly Father feeds them. **Are you not much more valuable than they?**"* (NIV, emphasis mine).

Do the birds of the air have to sow in order to reap? Do the birds of the air have to qualify for the Father to take care of them? No, they don't, and you are so much more valuable to Him than they are!

You're not a fearful slave to a law that tells you what you have to do to be blessed by your Heavenly Father. You're His beloved child, and He blesses you because you're a joint heir with Jesus!

So, let that truth sink down deep into your heart. Acknowledge the truth of what Jesus did for you, and say, "Father, thank you, for loving me! I'm not blessed because of anything I've done. I'm blessed because I am your son!" Live as a beloved son and watch the windows of heaven open up and pour you out so much blessing of peace, joy, provision, and abundance that you don't have room enough to receive it!

Oh, the joy of giving when you are truly free! After reading that Jesus set you free from the curse of the law, and that His blessing is poured out upon you—not because of what you do, but because of what He did for you—I hope you are dancing in the circle of His love with me!! I call it the FREEDOM dance! I've been set free, and I am never going back to religious bondage! I'm abundantly blessed because of Jesus, and so are you!

REFLECTION AND DISCUSSION QUESTIONS FOR CHAPTER 5

1. Have you ever been taught that you must tithe in order for God to bless you? Have you been afraid not to tithe? Did this cause you to give out of fear and obligation or out of love?

2. What did you learn from 1 John 4:16-18 about any teaching that produces fear in your heart? Does it come from love?

3. Read Galatians 3:13-14 again. Now that you understand that Jesus redeemed you from the curse of the law, what are your thoughts on Malachi 3:8-10?

4. According to Galatians 3:10, why do so many who depend on tithing to earn God's blessing end up so disappointed? Are you blessed because you tithe, or are you blessed because of Jesus?

5. What did you learn from Luke 18:9-15 about trusting in your good works to earn God's blessing? Who did Jesus bless—the one who trusted in his tithing or the one who received His mercy and grace?

6. Explain what you learned about New Covenant giving from 2 Corinthians 9:7-11.

7. Since you have been freed from any law or rule about giving, and you've been given the liberty to give from your heart, how will that affect the way you give?

8. What do you think Jesus was wanting you to learn by looking at the birds of the air? (Matthew 6:26).

Chapter 6
The Lie Religion Taught Me About God's Forgiveness

As a little girl, I remember being taught that even though I'd placed my faith in Jesus, my sins could still separate me from God. I was taught that I must continue to confess every sin to be forgiven by God. Like many others that were taught this in church, I went forward many times to confess my sins so that I might be forgiven and get right with God. This teaching never brought me peace and never changed my life. I looked around and saw the same people going forward every week, but never seeming to experience real change or victory in their lives.

Like all the other religious lies I had been taught, this one also produced fear in my heart: *What if I forget to confess one of my sins? What if Jesus comes back, or I die without confessing all my sins?*

When you live sin-conscious, there is no security in your salvation—only *fear* of losing it!

But 1 John 4:10,16 & 18 says, *"¹⁰This is love: He loved us long before we loved him. It was his love, not ours. He proved it by sending his Son to be the pleasing sacrificial offering to take away our sins... ¹⁶...God is love... ¹⁸Love NEVER brings fear, for fear is always related to punishment. But love's perfection drives the fear of punishment far from our hearts"* (TPT, emphasis mine).

God is love and love never brings fear! The Father, the Son, and the Holy Spirit—who was sent to guide us into all truth—never bring fear! The truth is, love drives all fear from our hearts and brings perfect peace. That's how we can always know if something we are taught is a lie. Does it produce fear? Then it's a lie! Does it produce peace? Then it's the truth!

Jesus is the Prince of Peace! 1 John 4:10 tells us that our Good Father loved us long before we loved Him. He proved how much He loved us by sending His Son to be the sacrificial offering to take away our sin.

All religious lies come from a misunderstanding or misinterpretation of scriptures. Usually, it comes from not rightly dividing the Word of Truth. That means, when we read the Scripture, we need to know who the Scripture is talking to. Is it referring to the Old Covenant or the New Covenant? Is it addressing an unbeliever or a believer?

Where Did This Lie Come From?

1 John 1:8-10:

> *"8If we say that we have no **sin**, we deceive ourselves, and the truth is not in us. 9If we **confess** our **sins**, He is faithful and just to forgive us our **sins** and to **cleanse** us from all **unrighteousness**. 10If we say that we have not sinned, we make Him a liar, and His word is not in us"* (NKJV, emphasis mine).

If you read this passage without complete understanding of the meaning of the words in these verses, it does sound like God will not forgive you until you confess every sin. However, in order to interpret these verses correctly, let us look at the true meaning of four of the words in this passage of Scripture.

It's important to understand that the Greek word for "sin" in verses 8 and 9 is a noun (Strong's G266). It is a state of being or an **identity**. The word for "sinned" in verse 10 is a verb (Strong's G264). It is the **action** of a person.

The word for "cleanse" in verse 9 means "to make clean; to free from defilement of sin and from faults; to free from guilt of sin; to purify" (Strong's G2511).

And the word for "unrighteousness" in verse 9 is also a noun (a state of being or an identity), and it means "a condition of not being right" (Strong's G93).

Since this verse is talking about sin as an **identity**, it obviously only applies to one who has not yet placed their faith in Christ—not specific actions. As an unbeliever, one must first acknowledge that he has sinned and is in need of a Savior before he will ever value the sacrifice Jesus made to take away his sins.

When we confessed that we have sinned, and placed our faith in Christ, this verse says that Jesus cleansed us from all unrighteousness. He cleansed us from the very identity of sin and gave us His perfect righteousness as our new identity. We were born again by the Spirit and became a new creature in Christ Jesus. We were cleansed from the condition of not being right and made righteous in Christ—one time and forever!

Contrary to what has been taught, 1 John 1:9 is a one-time salvation scripture. It is not a verse that teaches believers that we must make sure we confess every sin in order to be forgiven. If that were the case, there is no hope for any of us!

At one time or another, all of us have had unconfessed sin in our lives. It may have been fear, judgment, offence, jealousy or anger. When we recognize them, we turn from those actions, because it's not who we are in Jesus. But teaching a believer, "If you don't confess every sin, you won't be forgiven" is not sharing the truth of the Gospel. It produces fear and love NEVER brings fear!

The Truth That Set Me Free!

Colossians 2:13-14:

> *"13This "realm of death" describes our former state, for we were held in sin's grasp. But now, we've been resurrected out of that "realm of death" never to return, **for we are forever alive and forgiven of ALL our sins.** 14He canceled out every legal violation we had on our record and the old arrest warrant that stood to indict us. He erased it all— our sins, our stained soul—**he deleted it all and they cannot be retrieved!** Everything we once were in Adam has been placed onto his cross and nailed permanently there as a public display of cancellation"* (TPT, emphasis mine).

Did you hear that wonderful Good News? As a believer in Christ, you have been resurrected out of the realm of death, never to return. You are forever alive and forgiven of ALL your sins! He deleted ALL (your past, present, and future) sins and they cannot be retrieved! Everything you once were in Adam has been placed on the cross and nailed permanently there as a public display of cancellation! You are no longer defined as a sinner! The Good News is that your new identity is the righteousness of God in Christ Jesus!

This Good News is also found in 1 John 2:12:

> *"I remind you, dear children: your sins have been permanently removed because of the power of his name"* (TPT).

Did you hear that? Your sins have been PERMANTLY removed! Jesus removed the sin that had the power to define you by your bad behavior. He removed it by nailing it to the cross to set you free from all guilt and shame.

Romans 4:8, 23-25:

> *"⁸What happy progress comes to them when they hear the Lord speak over them, "I will never hold your sins against you!"*

> *"²³And this declaration was not just spoken over Abraham, ²⁴but also over us. For when we **believe** and **embrace** the one who brought our Lord Jesus back to life, perfect righteousness will be credited to our account as well. ²⁵Jesus was handed over to be crucified for the **forgiveness of our sins** and was raised back to life **to prove that he had made us right with God!**"* (TPT, emphasis mine).

The Good News makes you happy! Romans 4:8 says that when you hear your Good Father speak to your heart and say, "I will NEVER hold your sins against you!" your heart will be so happy! You know what that means? If what you believe about your Heavenly Father does not make your heart happy, then you're not believing the truth!

If you have placed your faith in Christ, to believe that you must continue to confess every sin in order to be forgiven is to devalue the sacrifice Jesus made for you! His one and final sacrifice was sufficient to forgive ALL your sins (past, present, and future) and cleanse you from all unrighteousness, one time and forever!

Romans 4:24-25 says that when we believe and embrace the one who brought our Lord Jesus back to life, perfect righteousness will be credited to our account. The truth of the Gospel is that you are no longer defined by your good or bad behavior! Your Heavenly Father's declaration over you in Christ is what defines you!

If He said He will NEVER hold your sins against you, then He will NEVER hold your sins against you! God is love, and 1 Corinthians 13:5 says that love does not keep record of your wrongs. You are forever forgiven in Christ!

I remember a teaching that my sister, Christy Rose, taught on forgiveness. She told the story of when she was at church camp and someone did something to her that was not very nice. Yet, in her heart she had no bad feelings toward that person because she was not holding that sin against them. When that person came up to her to apologize and ask for her forgiveness, she replied, "I've already forgiven you. I never held that against you." She had the heart of Jesus toward that person.

It reminded me of a time that something similar had happened to me. I had heard that someone I knew was talking bad about me behind my back. At the time, I understood that no one's judgment or criticism defines who I am. I am defined by my Heavenly Father's good opinion of me. He says I'm wonderful, good, and righteous in His sight. I am forgiven, and He is not holding any of my sins against me.

Because I had received His forgiveness in Christ, I was empowered to extend that same forgiveness toward the one who did me wrong. Whether or not they ever asked me to forgive them, in my heart I had already forgiven them and was not holding anything against them.

This is our true identity in Christ. It's an amazing life of freedom to not hold anything against anyone because your Heavenly Father isn't holding anything against you! One day that person came up to me and asked me to forgive them for saying those bad things about me, but I simply hugged them and said, "I think you're wonderful! I already forgave you!"

1 Corinthians 13:5 says that love holds no record of wrongs. That's how our Good Father is toward us. He holds no record of our wrongs and as He is so are we in this world! We are free to love and forgive because He first loved and forgave us! Ephesians 4:32 says to forgive one another, just as God through Christ has forgiven you.

The truth is, our sins have been permanently removed and have lost the power to define us—not because we've remembered to confess every last one of them, but because of the sacrifice of Jesus.

Hebrews 10:10-23:

> *"10By God's will **we have been purified and made holy once and for all** through the sacrifice of the body of Jesus, the Messiah!*
>
> *11Yet every day priests still serve, ritually offering the same sacrifices*

again and again—sacrifices that can never take away sin's guilt. ¹²*But when this Priest had offered the one supreme sacrifice for sin for all time he sat down on a throne at the right hand of God,* ¹³*waiting until all his whispering enemies are subdued and turn into his footstool.* ¹⁴*And by his one perfect sacrifice he* **made us perfectly holy and complete for all time***!*

¹⁵*The Holy Spirit confirms this to us by this Scripture, for the Lord says,* ¹⁶*"Afterwards, I will give them this covenant: I will embed my laws into their hearts and fasten my Word to their thoughts."* ¹⁷*And then he says, "I will not ever again remember their sins and lawless deeds!"* ¹⁸*So if* **our sins have been forgiven and forgotten***, why would we ever need to offer another sacrifice for sin?*

¹⁹*And now we are brothers and sisters in God's family because of the blood of Jesus, and he welcomes us to come right into the most holy sanctuary in the heavenly realm—boldly and with no hesitation.* ²⁰*For he has dedicated a new, life-giving way for us to approach God. For just as the veil was torn in two, Jesus' body was torn open to give us free and fresh access to him!*

²¹*And since we now have a magnificent King-Priest to welcome us into God's*

house, ²²we come closer to God and
*approach him with an open heart, **fully***
convinced by faith that nothing
will keep us at a distance from him.
For our hearts have been sprinkled with
*blood **to remove impurity and we***
have been freed from an accusing
conscience and now we are clean,
unstained, and presentable to God
inside and out!" (TPT, emphasis
mine).

²³*So let us seize and hold fast and retain*
without wavering the hope we cherish
and confess and our acknowledgement
of it, for He Who promised is reliable
(sure) and faithful to His word" (AMPC).

These verses reveal the wonderful promises our
Good Father has made to us in Christ. Look at Hebrews
10:23, again. I've always loved that verse, and I've
applied it to so many different promises in God's Word.

However, in context this verse is talking about the
promises God has made in this particular passage of
Scripture. So, let's apply this verse in our lives right
now. Let's value what Jesus did for us by
acknowledging it and confessing it to be true in our
lives. To confess means to say the same thing or to
agree with. So, let's agree with our Heavenly Father and
hold fast to what He has declared to be true about us:

❖ By God's will, I have been purified and made
   holy one time and forever through the
   sacrifice of Jesus (Hebrews 10:10).

❖ By His one perfect sacrifice, Jesus made me perfectly holy and complete for all time! (Hebrews 10:14).

❖ My Good Father has promised to write His Word about me on my heart and in my thoughts (Hebrews 10:16).

❖ My Good Father will never remember my sins! They are forgiven and forgotten! He will never hold my sins against me! (Hebrews 10:17; Romans 4:8).

❖ He welcomes me to come to Him boldly, with an open heart, and without hesitation. I am fully convinced that nothing can keep me at a distance from Him! Nothing can separate me from His love (Hebrews 10:19, 22).

❖ Jesus freed me from an accusing conscious and now I am clean, unstained, and presentable to my Father inside and out! (Hebrews 10:22; Romans 8:39).

For many years of my Christian life, I did not know this wonderful Good News. Religion had taught me to focus on my sin instead of Jesus. When you understand your Heavenly Father is not holding anything against you, you will come to Him without any hesitation. He welcomes you to come to him boldly, with an open heart, to share all your fears, all your concerns, and all your struggles—without feeling guilty or ashamed in any way.

He is a Good, Good Father. He is the Daddy you've always wanted. The one who will love you in the middle of your mess, look at you and say, "I'm not holding anything against you! I will never remember your sins!

I will write My Word upon your heart and remind you who you are." In those moments, He will remind you that your sins are forgiven, and you have been made the righteousness of God in Christ. 2 Peter 2:9 says that when we don't act right, it's because we have forgotten that all our sins have been forgiven.

In Luke 7:36-50, a story is told of a woman who washes Jesus' feet with her hair. She was so thankful for the forgiveness He had given her that she expressed great love for Him in that way. In referring to this woman, Jesus said, "She has been forgiven much, so she loves much!"

When you realize how much Jesus has forgiven you, it changes your life and you love much! The power of forgiveness removes judgment and condemnation from your heart and you begin to love Jesus and love others with a new-found freedom. You no longer hold anything in your heart against anyone because you know that your Heavenly Father is not holding anything in His heart against you. You have been completely forgiven so you are empowered to forgive others.

This truth has the power to heal your relationship with your spouse, your children, your friends, and even your enemies! There are people who claim that teaching others that the Father is not holding anyone's sins against them, and that ALL their sins have been forgiven, will cause them to go out and sin. These people simply do not understand the power of forgiveness!

When I realized ALL my sins—past, present, and future—were forgiven, and that Jesus had given me the beautiful gift of righteousness, I fell deeply in love with Him! His love transformed my heart and brought the fruit of His Spirit out in my life. That's what will happen to anyone who understands and embraces this beautiful gift of forgiveness. They will fall in love with Jesus, and His love will transform their lives!

Jesus Set You Free From an Accusing Conscious

Hebrews 10:22 says that our hearts have been sprinkled with blood to remove impurity and we have been freed from an accusing conscience. Romans 8:1 says, *"So now **the case is closed**. There remains no accusing voice of condemnation against those who are joined in life-union with Jesus..."* (TPT, emphasis mine).

So, there is no more accusing voices for us when we fail. We've all failed and we've all messed up. Those accusing voices try to get us to believe, "You're a failure!" When that happens, we can turn our thoughts to Jesus and remember that all our sins are forgiven.

Jesus came so you would never have to live under another accusing voice ever again. That's how much He loved you! And since you're not accused, you are free not to accuse anyone else. Since you're not condemned, you are free not to condemn anyone else. Since you're not judged, you are free not to judge anyone else. You're finally free from all guilt and shame because you are forgiven, and you can extend that forgiveness to everyone around you. That's the free life Jesus came to give us! A life of love! You can live in that freedom simply by receiving His forgiveness and the gift of righteousness every single day of your life.

Repent and Believe the Good News

Those who oppose the Good News that all our sins (past, present, and future) are forgiven usually bring up the truth that Jesus told us we must repent. Let's take a look at what Jesus meant when He said that.

Mark 1:14-15:

> "*14Jesus went into Galilee, proclaiming the good news of God. 15"The time has come," he said. "The kingdom of God has come near. **Repent** and believe the good news!"*" (NIV, emphasis mine).

Jesus was preaching the Gospel of the kingdom of God. He said the kingdom of God is at hand. Romans 14:17 tells us that the kingdom of God is righteousness, peace, and joy in the Holy Spirit. It is the Good News of righteousness given to us as a free gift.

This word repent in Mark 1:15 means "to change one's mind" (Strong's 3340). True repentance is not asking for forgiveness over and over again, as some have taught. Rather, it is changing your mind. It means to change what you believe about God and about yourself. So, if you fail, and you find yourself feeling guilty or condemned in your mind—**repent**! Change your focus from your failures to Jesus and believe the Good News.

What is the Good News That Jesus Wants You to Believe?

Colossians 1:13-14; 22-23:

> *"13For he has rescued us from the kingdom of darkness and transferred us into the Kingdom of his dear Son, 14who purchased our freedom and forgave our sins.*
>
> *22Yet now he has reconciled you to himself through the death of Christ in his physical body. As a result, he has brought you into his own presence, and you are holy and blameless as you stand before him without a single fault. 23But you must continue to believe this truth and stand firmly in it. Don't drift away from the assurance you received when you heard the Good News"* (NLT).

This passage of Scripture clearly describes the Good News of the Kingdom of God that Jesus wants you to believe. He wants you to believe that ALL your sins have been forgiven and the Father has reconciled you to Himself. Jesus wants you to believe that you are holy and blameless as you stand before the Father, without a single fault. He wants you to BELIEVE this truth and stand in it firmly. Don't drift away from the assurance you received when you heard this Good News!

If you aren't believing the Good News that ALL your sins (past, present, and future) have been forgiven and that you stand before God holy, blameless and without a single fault, Jesus said that it's time to repent—change your mind—and believe the Good News!

All bad behavior comes from not believing the Good News about who you are in Christ. So, the next time you find yourself behaving badly—repent! Turn your focus to Jesus, and let God change the way you think about Him and about yourself. Believe the Good News!

Stand firm in the truth and declare it to be true in your life:

"Heavenly Father, thank You for rescuing me from the kingdom of darkness, bringing me into the kingdom of Your Son and forgiving all my sins! Thank you for loving me so much! I am holy and blameless as I stand before You, without a single fault! You do not hold any of my sins against me, and I do not hold any sins against others, either. Because of Jesus, I am free from every accusing voice toward myself, and every accusing voice toward others! I am just like Jesus in this world! Thank you for your gift of forgiveness!"

Now, go be who you are in Him! Embrace the gift of forgiveness and enjoy the life of freedom that Jesus died to give you!

REFLECTION AND DISCUSSION
QUESTIONS FOR CHAPTER 6

1. Have you ever been taught that you must confess every sin if you want God to forgive you? If that were the truth, would you have security in your salvation? What if you forgot to confess a sin or died with unconfessed sin? What fruit does this teaching produce in a person's heart?

2. Read 1 John 4:10, 16, 18 again. What do these verses tell us about God? How can we discern whether a teaching we hear is a lie or the truth?

3. How have people misunderstood or misinterpreted 1 John 1:8-10? Now that you know the true meaning of the words sin, cleanse, and unrighteousness, what is the true meaning of these verses? Is this a one-time salvation passage, or a teaching to believers to continue to confess every sin?

4. Discuss the truth found in Colossians 2:13-14. What Good News has been proclaimed in these verses?

5. Read 1 John 2:12 again. What does permanently mean?

6. What did your Good Father promise you in Romans 4:8? Why was Jesus handed over to be crucified and why was He raised to life again? What did His finished work provide for you?

7. Read Hebrews 10:10-23 again. Discuss the Good News found in these verses. Verse 23 tells you to hold fast to and confess the promises found in this passage of Scripture. Take time right now to acknowledge what Jesus' sacrifice provided for you. Why is this such Good News?

8. In Mark 1:14-15 Jesus tells us to repent and believe the Good News. What is true repentance? According to Colossians 1:13-23, what is the Good News that Jesus wants you to believe?

Chapter 7
The Lie Religion Teaches About God's Discipline

Throughout my life, I have heard many lies religion has taught about God's discipline. I have heard messages that God is angry when people act badly. I have even heard people teach that God uses bad circumstances, such as natural disasters and even sickness, to discipline His children. People have actually believed that God is punishing them for their sins.

How can we know that theses teachings are lies? Because, just like all the other lies religion has taught, this teaching creates fear in our hearts. And any teaching that produces fear is a lie because God never brings fear!

Again, 1 John 4:16 and 18 says:

> *"16...God is love... 18Love NEVER **brings**
> **fear**, for fear is always related to
> punishment. But love's perfection drives
> the fear of punishment far from our
> hearts. Whoever walks constantly
> afraid of punishment has not reached
> love's perfection"* (TPT, emphasis mine).

I don't think it can get any clearer than that. Let's
really think about what these verses are saying. God is
love! Love **NEVER** brings fear. Fear is **ALWAYS** related to
punishment. But love's perfection drives the fear of
punishment far from our hearts! So, if we are afraid that
God will punish us, we have been held in bondage to a
lie that religion has taught us. We really don't know God
and have not fully understood His perfect Love for us.

The Truth That Set Me Free!

In the last chapter, we learned from Romans 4:8 that
our Good Father will **NEVER** hold our sins against us.
When you placed your faith in Jesus, you became the
righteousness of God in Christ. Your Good Father sees
you as perfect, righteous, and without fault in His eyes,
and He will never change His opinion of you. And He has
promised to never be angry at you. When we act badly,
He corrects us, not by telling us how bad we are, but by
reminding us who we are. He corrects the wrong belief of
our hearts concerning who He is and who we are in Jesus.

Hebrews 12:5-12 says:

> *"5And have you forgotten his **encouraging**
> **words** spoken to you as his children? He*

said, "My child, don't underestimate the value of the **discipline and training** of the Lord God, or get depressed when he has to **correct you**. *6For the **Lord's training** of your life is the **evidence of his faithful love**. And when he draws you to himself, it proves you are his **delightful child**."

*7Fully embrace God's **correction** as part of your training, for he is doing what any loving father does for his children. For who has ever heard of a child who never had to be corrected? *8We all should **welcome God's discipline as the validation of authentic sonship**. For if we have never once endured his correction it only proves we are strangers and not sons.

*9And isn't it true that we respect our earthly fathers even though they corrected and disciplined us? Then we should demonstrate an even greater respect for God, our spiritual Father, **as we submit to his life-giving discipline**. *10Our parents corrected us for the short time of our childhood as it seemed good to them. But **God corrects us throughout our lives for our own good, giving us an invitation to share his holiness**. *11Now all discipline seems to be more pain than pleasure at the time, yet later **it will produce a transformation of character**, bringing a harvest of **righteousness and peace** to those who yield to it" (TPT, emphasis mine).

I love this passage of Scripture! It so beautifully describes the truth about how our Good Father disciplines us. In verse 5, we see that His discipline and correction is always encouraging! Verse 6 says that when your Heavenly Father corrects you it's proof of His faithful love for you. He draws you to Himself and reminds you who you are to prove that you are His delightful child. Verses 7-9 encourages you to embrace His correction, because He loves you and wants you to experience His life.

His discipline is never condemning, but always life-giving. Verse 10 says that God corrects you throughout your whole life for your good, giving you an invitation to share in His peace, joy, and love. He's inviting you to share His life. When you yield to His correction, verse 11 says it will produce a harvest of righteousness and peace in your life. The fruit of who you really are will come out for all to see!

Religion Focuses on Behavior Modification— Jesus Focuses On Heart Transformation

To fully understand the truth about the discipline and correction of your Good Father, let's look at the context of Hebrews 12:5-11. Hebrews 11 is talking about people who believed God. It says that Abel, Enoch, Noah, Abraham, Sarah, Isaac, Jacob, Joseph, Moses, and Rahab believed what God said about them and they experienced His good plan for their lives.

Then Hebrews 12:1-2 goes on to say that these men and women are witnesses to a life of believing God and encourages us to do the same:

*"¹Therefore, since we are surrounded by such a huge crowd of witnesses **to the life of faith**, let us strip off every weight that slows us down, especially **the sin** that so easily trips us up. And let us run with endurance the race God has set before us. ²**We do this by keeping our eyes on Jesus**, the champion who initiates and perfects our faith"* (NLT, emphasis mine).

The whole book of Hebrews addresses the sin of unbelief, which is not believing what our Good Father says about us in Christ. Hebrews 3:12, 17, and 19 makes this very clear:

"¹²So search your hearts every day, my brothers and sisters, and make sure that none of you has evil or unbelief hiding within you. For it will lead you astray, and make you unresponsive to the living God.

*¹⁷They grieved God for forty years **by sinning in their unbelief**...*

*¹⁹It is clear that they could not enter into their inheritance because they wrapped their hearts in **unbelief**"* (TPT, emphasis mine).

Hebrews 12:1-2 tells us to strip off the sin of unbelief by keeping our eyes on Jesus. When we keep our eyes on Jesus and believe the truth that all our sins are forgiven, and we've been made righteous in Him, it produces the fruit of the Spirit in our lives.

However, when we are not believing who we are in Christ, we experience fear, worry, anger, judgment, jealousy, and all kinds of bad behavior. That's when our loving Father corrects the belief of our hearts. Remember, when our Heavenly Father corrects us, He doesn't point out our sin and tell us how bad we are. Instead, He points us to Jesus and reminds us who we are and the promises we have in Him. He wants us to believe who we are in Jesus so that we can experience His life within us.

When I am not believing who I am in Jesus, negative emotions rise up in my soul, and this often results in bad behavior. Let me share an example from my own life.

Several years ago, I had a dream in my heart to own lodges in Branson, MO and holding Because of Jesus Ministries conferences and retreats there. When my husband and I were going through the process of purchasing our first lodge, we faced many challenges.

One day, when I was out to lunch with some of my friends, I got a phone call from my husband telling me that the mortgage company we were working with was not going to accept the information we gave them to approve us for the loan. All of a sudden, all kinds of negative emotions began to rise up in my heart.

I felt anger toward the mortgage company and the people we were working with. I felt fear, frustration, and disappointment that it might not work out the way I had hoped. I was feeling all these negative emotions because, in that moment, I wasn't believing who I am or what my Good Father said about me.

Now, my wonderful Jesus friends were with me that day, and my Good Father used my friend, Sherry, to bring correction to the unbelief of my heart.

My Good Father has corrected me in different ways. Sometimes it's through a message or a scripture. Sometimes it's His sweet voice speaking to my heart. But this time, His correction came through a sweet friend. One thing is for sure, His correction is always encouraging, never condemning, and always life-giving. My friend, Sherry, spoke life-giving words to me by reminding me of what my Good Father said about me in Psalm 138:8. She said, "Connie, the Lord will perfect that which concerns you." In that moment, I heard the sweet sound of correction.

I realized I was not experiencing the life of God. Anger, judgment, fear, and frustration is not the life of God. All those negative emotions were happening within me because I was not believing what my Heavenly Father said about me.

Hebrews 12:11 says that when we yield to our Good Father's correction, it produces a harvest of peace in those who will be trained by it. When my friend, Sherry, reminded me of the truth that had the power to set me free, I had a choice to yield to that loving correction or to reject it.

And I've done both! I've rejected God's correction and held onto my own opinion, and that brought me emotional pain. I've also yielded to God's correction and it brought me peace.

Thankfully, this day I yielded to His correction by giving up my opinion of the situation and embracing the truth that the Lord would perfect that which concerns me. I can remember the drive home as I continued to talk to my Good Father and thank Him for loving me and showing me the truth that set me free from fear, anger, and frustration.

That day I turned my eyes upon Jesus, the author and finisher of my faith (Hebrews 12:2). I could feel faith rising up within me as I embraced His loving words to me. He had corrected the belief of my heart, and just like Hebrews 12:11 teaches, when I yielded to His loving correction, I began to experience joy, peace and hope once again.

That very day, after I got home, I discovered the Father had worked that situation out so beautifully that we didn't even need that mortgage company to buy the piece of property. We were able to pay cash for that first lodge and my dream to hold ministry retreats and conferences came to pass. That was God's plan for me all along, and He just wanted me to accept His correction and His discipline so that I could experience His wonderful plan for my life.

3 Truths About Our Father's Discipline and Correction

1. Your Good Father has promised to never be angry at you or punish you!

In Isaiah 54:9-10, He made a promise to you and I:

> *"9I swear that I will never again be angry and punish you"* (NLT).

"¹⁰Though the mountains be shaken and the hills be removed, yet my unfailing love for you will not be shaken nor my covenant of peace be removed,' says the Lord, who has compassion on you" (NIV).

I absolutely love this promise from our Good Father. It causes me to run to Him when I'm struggling or when I have failed because I know He promised that He will never be angry with me or punish me. That day, when I was having a bad attitude and I was feeling angry and critical toward those people, my loving Father looked at me and saw how the belief of my heart was causing me emotional pain. With a heart of compassion, He lovingly corrected the belief of my heart so that I could believe the truth and experience His peace.

Religion has taught that God is angry at people when they sin, but whoever teaches that is teaching a lie because He made a covenant promise through Jesus in Isaiah 54:9-10 to never be angry or punish us. Let's believe Him! His unfailing love for us will never fail!

2. Trials are not God's Discipline. Only that which is good comes from Him!

James 1:12-17 says:

*"¹²God blesses those who patiently endure testing and temptation. Afterward they will receive the crown of life that God has promised to those who love him. ¹³And remember, when you are being tempted, **do not say, "God is***

tempting me." God is never tempted to do wrong, and he never tempts anyone else. ¹⁴Temptation comes from our own desires, which entice us and drag us away. ¹⁵These desires give birth to sinful actions. And when sin is allowed to grow, it gives birth to death" (NLT, emphasis mine).

*¹⁶**Don't be deceived**, my dear brothers and sisters. ¹⁷Every good and perfect gift is from above, coming down from the Father of the heavenly lights, who does not change like shifting shadows"* (NIV, emphasis mine).

When I read these verses, it's hard to believe that religion was ever able to deceive anyone into believing that trials are God's discipline. We all know that negative circumstances such as sickness, natural disasters, and financial struggles all tempt us to be discouraged, angry or worried. If God is the one sending them, then He is the one tempting us.

However, James 1:13 says that when you are being tempted, do not say, **"God is tempting me," because God never tempts anyone.** Verse 16 warns us to not be deceived into believing that negative circumstances come from God. The truth is, He is a Good Father and only that which good and perfect comes from Him.

3. Your Good Father is training you in righteousness.

2 Timothy 3:16 says, *"All Scripture is inspired by God and profitable for teaching, for reproof, for correction, for training in righteousness"* (NASB).

All Scripture is inspired by God to teach us, correct any wrong beliefs of our hearts, and train us in who we are in Christ. We are righteous, good, loving, kind, generous, blessed and complete in Christ! When our behavior does not reflect our true identities, our Good Father corrects the beliefs of our hearts by reminding us who we are through His Word. That day when I responded badly to the bad news from the mortgage company, He corrected the belief of my heart by reminding me that He will perfect everything that concerns me. He was training me in righteousness.

Believing the Truth Produces Good Fruit

2 Peter 1:3-9 says:

> *"3By his divine power, God has given us everything we need for living a godly life. We have received all of this by coming to know him, the one who called us to himself by means of his marvelous glory and excellence. 4And because of his glory and excellence, he has given us great and precious promises. These are the promises that enable you to share his divine nature and escape the world's corruption caused by human desires.*
>
> *5In view of all this, make every effort to* **respond to God's promises**. *Supplement your faith with a generous provision of* **moral excellence**, *and moral excellence with* **knowledge**, *6and knowledge with* **self-control**, *and*

> *self-control with **patient endurance,**
> and patient endurance with **godliness,**
> 7and godliness with **brotherly**
> **affection,** and brotherly affection with
> **love for everyone.***
>
> *8The more you grow like this, the more
> productive and useful you will be in your
> knowledge of our Lord Jesus Christ. 9But
> those who fail to develop in this way are
> shortsighted or blind, **forgetting that**
> **they have been cleansed from their**
> **old sins**"* (NLT, emphasis mine).

Our Good Father has given us great and precious promises in Christ so that we can escape the corruption that is in this world—including greed, fear, anger, division, judgment, offense, and jealousy—and partake of His divine nature of love, joy, and peace. He's promised us the gift of forgiveness and His perfect righteousness. He's promised to never stop loving us and to never hold our sins against us. He's promised to take care of us, prosper us, rescue our children, and work all things together for our good.

2 Peter 1:5-7 tells us to make every effort to respond to God's promises. When we respond to God's promises, moral excellence, knowledge, self-control, patience, godliness, brotherly affection, and love for everyone is the fruit of our lives. But verse 9 says if this fruit isn't coming out in our life it's because we have forgotten that all our sins have been forgiven.

It's important to understand that the Greek word for "sins" in verse 9 is a noun (Strong's G266). It is a state of being or an identity. This verse is saying that if our lives are not bearing good fruit, it's because we have forgotten that all our sins have been forgiven and that we've been made the righteousness of God in Christ. We have forgotten who we are in Christ, and the promises we have in Him.

It's in these moments that our loving Father corrects the beliefs of our hearts by reminding us who we are in Jesus! When we understand God's loving discipline, we don't run from it, we welcome it. It's the sweet sound of correction because He loves us, and He doesn't want us to live in emotional pain. He wants us to experience abundant life.

For example, when I responded to God's promise that He would perfect that which concerns me, I escaped the emotional pain of fear, anger, judgment, and frustration, and I partook of His perfect peace. He corrected the belief of my heart, and it produced the fruit of righteousness in my life.

The Sweet Sound of Correction: A Case of Mistaken Identity

There is a story in the Bible that Jesus tells which perfectly reveals the true nature of our Good Father and how He disciplines and corrects His children. It is the story of two sons who were behaving badly. In both cases, the Father corrected the beliefs of each son's heart by reminding him of his true identity as His son.

Luke 15:11-24:

> *"11Then Jesus said, "Once there was a father with two sons. 12The younger son*

came to his father and said, 'Father, don't you think it's time to give me the share of your estate that belongs to me?' So the father went ahead and distributed among the two sons their inheritance.

13Shortly afterward, the younger son packed up all his belongings and traveled off to see the world. He journeyed to a far-off land where he soon wasted all he was given in a binge of extravagant and reckless living.

14With everything spent and nothing left, he grew hungry, for there was a severe famine in that land. 15So he begged a farmer in that country to hire him. The farmer hired him and sent him out to feed the pigs. 16The son was so famished, he was willing to even eat the slop given to the pigs, because no one would feed him a thing.

17Humiliated, the son finally realized what he was doing and he thought, 'There are many workers at my father's house who have all the food they want with plenty to spare. **They lack nothing**. Why am I here dying of hunger, feeding these pigs and eating their slop? 18I want to go back home to my father's house, and I'll say to him, "Father, I was wrong. I have sinned against you. 19I'll never be worthy to be called your son. Please, Father, just treat me like one of your employees."

²⁰*So the young son set off for home.*
From a long distance away, his father
saw him coming, dressed as a
beggar, and **great compassion**
swelled up in his heart for his son
who was returning home. So the
father raced out to meet him. He
swept him up in his arms, hugged
him dearly, and kissed him over
and over with tender love.

²¹*Then the son said, 'Father, I was*
wrong. I have sinned against you. I
could never deserve to be called your
son. Just let me be—'

The father interrupted and said, **'Son,**
you're home now!'

²²*Turning to his servants, the father*
said, 'Quick, bring me the best robe, **my**
very own robe, *and I will place it on*
his shoulders. Bring the ring, the seal of
sonship, and I will put it on his finger.
And bring out the best shoes you can find
for my son. ²³*Let's prepare a great feast*
and celebrate. ²⁴*For this beloved son of*
mine was once dead, but now he's alive
again. Once he was lost, but now he is
found!' And everyone celebrated with
overflowing joy" (TPT, emphasis mine).

The younger son went out into the world and
wasted his inheritance on extravagant and reckless
living. He acted badly. He slept with prostitutes and
ended up in the pigpen—hungry, broke and rejected.

Now. religion would say that this was the Father's punishment for the bad things he had done. But the Father had nothing to do with the negative circumstances his son was experiencing. Those circumstances were the result of a wrong belief of his heart. He believed something about himself and his Father that was not true. His bad actions caused him to believe that he was no longer worthy to be a son and that he had to pay for his mistakes.

However, when his Father saw the emotional pain he was in because of the wrong belief of his heart, great compassion swelled up in his heart for his son. That reminds me of Isaiah 54:10, where our Father promised to never be angry or punish us, but to only have compassion toward us.

Here it is demonstrated so beautifully in this story. With great compassion, his Father raced out to meet him. He swept him up in his arms and embraced him, kissing him over and over with tender love. Before His son could even speak a word, the Father fully embraced his son. The son tried to tell the Father how unworthy he was because of his bad actions and that he didn't deserve to be his son, but his Father quickly interrupted him, and said, **"Son, you're home now."**

The son had lost sight of his true identity, and it caused him to act badly. The Father corrected the belief of his heart by reminding him of the truth. Turning to his servants, the Father said, "Quick, bring me the best robe, my very own robe. Remind my son that he is righteous. Put the ring on his finger and remind him that he will always be my son. Bring the best shoes and put them on his feet. Slaughter the calf and remind my son that I'm not holding any of his sins against him. Let's prepare a great feast and celebrate, for this beloved son of mine has come home!"

What a beautiful picture of the loving discipline and correction of our Good Father. It's always about correcting the beliefs of our hearts. When we receive His correction and believe who we truly are in Jesus, it produces a harvest of righteousness in our lives.

Now let's finish reading this story, in Luke 15:25-32, to see how the Father corrected the bad behavior of the older son in the very same way:

> *"25Now, the older son was out working in the field when his brother returned, and as he approached the house he heard the music of celebration and dancing. 26So he called over one of the servants and asked, 'What's going on?'*
>
> *27The servant replied, 'It's your younger brother. He's returned home and your father is throwing a party to celebrate his homecoming.'*
>
> ***28The older son became angry and refused to go in and celebrate.*** *So his father came out and pleaded with him, 'Come and enjoy the feast with us!'*
>
> *29The son said, 'Father, listen! How many years have I been working like a slave for you, performing every duty you've asked as a faithful son? And I've never once disobeyed you. But you've*

never thrown a party for me because of my faithfulness. Never once have you even given me a goat that I could feast on and celebrate with my friends like he's doing now. 30But look at this son of yours! He comes back after wasting your wealth on prostitutes and reckless living, and here you are throwing a great feast to celebrate—for him!'

31The father said, 'My son, you are always with me by my side. Everything I have is yours to enjoy. 32It's only right to celebrate like this and be overjoyed, because this brother of yours was once dead and gone, but now he is alive and back with us again. He was lost but now he is found!'" (TPT, emphasis mine).

The older son was also behaving badly. He had anger and jealousy in his heart. He was self-righteous and judgmental toward his younger brother, thinking he was better than him. That's what religion does to the human heart. It causes us to focus on our faithfulness instead of God's. It causes us to be judgmental and critical toward others.

The older son acted like this because of a wrong belief of his heart. He saw himself as a servant instead of a son. He believed his actions made him deserving of his Father's blessing and approval. But the Father corrected that wrong belief in his heart by saying, **"My son, you are always with me and everything I have is already yours to enjoy!"**

Contrary to what religion has taught about God's discipline, this story makes it so clear that our Good Father is never angry at us, nor does He bring bad circumstances into our lives to discipline us when we act badly. Instead, when He sees that our wrong beliefs about ourselves are causing us emotional pain, His heart is full of compassion and love toward us. He corrected the beliefs of both of these son's hearts and reminded them of their true identities, and that's exactly what He does with us.

Religion focuses on our bad behavior, but our Good Father corrects the beliefs of our hearts. Believing lies produces bad behavior but believing the truth about who you are in Christ produces good fruit!

So, my brothers and sisters in Christ, when you are feeling negative emotions or have acted badly, listen for the sweet sound of correction, and let your Good Father correct the belief of your heart. Humbly, receive His loving correction.

There's no condemnation to those who are in Christ Jesus. You never have to feel condemned or ashamed when the Father corrects you. Your Good Father loves you, and He wants you to experience His life. Just simply yield to His loving correction, and believe what He says about you, and you will experience a harvest of righteousness and peace in your life!

REFLECTION AND DISCUSSION
QUESTIONS FOR CHAPTER 7

1. Have you ever been taught or believed that God is angry at you when you act badly? Have you ever heard a message that God uses bad circumstances, such as natural disasters or sickness, to discipline His children? How did these beliefs make your heart feel?

2. 1 John 4:16-18 is one of our foundational scriptures for this study. What is the litmus test for whether or not what you hear is the truth? Does a teaching that comes from God ever produce fear? When a person believes they are loved by God, how does it affect their heart?

3. What did you learn about God's discipline in Hebrews 12:5-12? When you yield to the sweet sound of your Father's correction, what will it produce in your life?

4. When you consider the context of Hebrews 12:5-12, what is it that your Good Father is correcting when He disciplines you? How do we strip off every wrong belief that holds us back? (Hebrews 12:1-2).

5. What did God promise you in Isaiah 54:9-10? How does this make your heart feel?

6. In James 1:12-17, what did the Holy Spirit tell you to never say when you are being tried or tempted by a negative circumstance in your life? Do negative circumstances come from God? Why or why not?

7. When your Good Father corrects the belief of your heart with His Word, what is He teaching you? (2 Timothy 3:16).

8. According to 2 Peter 1:3-9, what does believing the truth produce in your life? If you are acting badly, what have you forgotten?

9. You learned in this chapter that when you act badly it is a case of mistaken identity. Your Good Father corrects the wrong belief of your heart. It's the sweet sound of correction because of His great love for you! What did you learn about how your Good Father corrects bad behavior in the story about the 2 sons found in Luke 15:11-32?

Chapter 8
Religion Says Do! Jesus Says Done!

I've lost track of the number of messages I've heard over the years about what I needed to do if I wanted God to bless my finances, answer my prayers, heal my body, or bless my life. The lie religion taught me was that I had to "do" something if I wanted to receive God's approval and blessing.

The do-do list goes on and on, but this list of rules—that would supposedly earn me God's approval and blessing—never ended! The list just kept growing! When I attempted to "do" what supposedly qualified me, and somewhat succeeded, I found myself judging others who didn't.

When I attempted to do the do-do list and I failed, I found myself feeling like I'd never be good enough! Oh, the bondage of focusing on yourself—a human attempt to make yourself right before God through your list of religious rules!

BUT! Oh, the freedom of focusing on Jesus and embracing the truth that we have been made perfectly righteous as a gift of His grace! We are approved and blessed, not because of what we have done, but because of what Jesus has done for us!

Man-made religion focuses on man's behavior as the way to God's blessing and approval. It's a fake gospel because the focus is not on what Jesus did, but rather on what man must do. This story is far too common in religious circles: A person begins their faith journey by trusting Jesus for salvation, but then they are handed a long list of religious rules to follow in order to be a good Christian, get their prayers answered, find favor, and be blessed by God! Although Jesus and what He did for them started out as the focus, it quickly turned from what **Jesus** did for **them** to what **they** need to do for **Him**.

The Apostle Paul Warned Us Not to Fall for This Religious Lie

Galatians 1:6-7:

> *"⁶I am shocked over how quickly you have strayed away from the Anointed One who called you to himself by his loving mercy. I'm frankly astounded that you now embrace a distorted gospel! ⁷That is a fake "gospel" that is simply not true. There is only one gospel—the gospel*

of the Messiah! Yet you have allowed those who mingle law with grace to confuse you with lies" (TPT).

Galatians 2:4-5:

"4I met with them privately and confidentially because false "brothers" had been secretly smuggled into the church meetings. They were sent to spy on the wonderful liberty and freedom that we have in Jesus. Their agenda was to bring us back into the legalistic bondage of religion. 5But you must know that we did not submit to their religious shackles not even for a moment, so that we might keep the gospel of grace unadulterated for you" (TPT).

The Galatians had heard the true Gospel that they were forgiven and made righteous because of what Jesus did, and then some religious teachers were attempting to pull them back into the bondage of trying to earn what God had freely given by His grace.

There are two messages that are presented as the Gospel in the church today. One is a fake gospel that focuses on man. The other is the true Gospel that focuses on Jesus. Every time you hear a message, you are either going to hear the fake gospel or the true Gospel. If the message you hear is pointing you to what you need to do, it's the fake Gospel that puts you in bondage to your own human effort. However, if it's pointing you to Jesus and what He has done, it's the true Gospel that sets you free!

The Truth That Set Me Free!

What is the TRUE Gospel that the Apostle Paul taught? He made it very clear in Galatians 2:16, 18-21:

> "*16We know full well that we don't receive God's perfect righteousness as a reward for keeping the law, but by the faith of Jesus, the Messiah! His faithfulness, not ours, has saved us, and we have received God's perfect righteousness. **Now we know that God accepts no one by the keeping of religious laws!***
>
> *18For if I start over and reconstruct the old religious system that I have torn down with the message of grace, I will appear to be one who turns his back on the truth.*
>
> *19But because the Messiah lives in me, I've now died to the law's dominion over me so that I can live for God.*
>
> *20**My old identity has been co-crucified with Messiah and no longer lives**; for the nails of his cross crucified me with him. And now the essence of this new life is no longer mine, **for the Anointed One lives his life through me—we live in union as one! My new life is empowered by the faith of the Son of God who loves me so much that he gave himself for me, and dispenses his life into mine!***

> **²¹*So that is why I don't view God's grace***
> ***as something minor or peripheral. For if***
> ***keeping the law could release God's***
> ***righteousness to us, the Anointed One***
> ***would have died for nothing*** (TPT,
> emphasis mine).

I love this passage of Scripture! The Apostle Paul makes it so clear in verse 16 that we don't receive God's perfect righteousness as a reward for keeping the law, but we receive it by the faith of Jesus! It was His faithfulness that made us righteous, not ours! WOW! The fake gospel (religion) focuses on the faithfulness of man, but the true Gospel focuses on the faithfulness of Jesus!

In verse 18, the Apostle Paul said that if he began to teach that you had to keep religious laws in order to be righteous and blessed by God, He would be turning his back on the truth.

For example, if I began to teach you that you had to do something in order to qualify yourself for God's provision, to be healed, or to be favored by God, I would be turning my back on the truth. I would be taking your eyes off of Jesus and His faithfulness and pointing you to yours. God's gift of **perfect righteousness** is standing approved, blameless, perfect, holy, qualified, blessed, favored and without fault in His eyes because of what Jesus did, not because of what you do!

The Apostle Paul goes on to say in verse 19-20 that because Jesus lives in him, he died to the law's demands on him so that he could truly live for God. The law demands that we obey it perfectly in order to qualify for God's blessing. We absolutely know that no one can meet the demands of the law.

But, just like the Apostle Paul, you and I died to the law's demands on us when we were crucified in Christ. The law no longer has the power to condemn us or define us. Our old identities died with Him and we've been resurrected to brand new lives. We are one with Jesus and He lives His life through us! Our new life is empowered by embracing what Jesus believes about us! He loves us, and He dispenses His life into ours! Now that's the true Gospel!

The True Gospel is summed up in verse 21. If we could follow a do-do list to be made righteous and blessed by God, then Jesus died for nothing! If we could qualify ourselves, we wouldn't have needed a Savior. All we would have needed was a law to follow.

But none of us could ever qualify ourselves by keeping the law perfectly. That's why Jesus came to qualify us as a gift of His grace. We do not set aside or devalue this gift by trying to earn it by our human effort. **Anyone who still believes that they are blessed because of what they do has devalued and set aside the grace of God.**

In order to get an even clearer understanding of the true Gospel, let's read Galatians 2:16, 19-21 again in The Message translation:

> *"...16We know very well that we are not set right with God by rule-keeping but only through personal faith in Jesus Christ. How do we know? We tried it— and we had the best system of rules the*

world has ever seen! Convinced that no human being can please God by self-improvement, we believed in Jesus as the Messiah so that we might be set right before God by trusting in the Messiah, not by trying to be good.

19-21 What actually took place is this: I tried keeping rules and working my head off to please God, and it didn't work. So I quit being a "law man" so that I could be God's man. 20 Christ's life showed me how, and enabled me to do it. I identified myself completely with him. Indeed, I have been crucified with Christ. My ego is no longer central. It is no longer important that I appear righteous before you or have your good opinion, and I am no longer driven to impress God. Christ lives in me. The life you see me living is not "mine," but it is lived by faith in the Son of God, who loved me and gave himself for me. I am not going to go back on that.

Is it not clear to you that to go back to that old rule-keeping, peer-pleasing religion would be an abandonment of everything personal and free in my relationship with God? I refuse to do that, to repudiate God's grace. If a living relationship with God could come by rule-keeping, then Christ died unnecessarily."

Wow! The true Good News couldn't be any clearer. This passage of Scripture says we know very well that we are not set right with God by rule-keeping, but by personal faith in Jesus. I can so relate to these verses. They are my personal testimony of breaking free from the lies of religion and embracing my true identity in Christ. Just like the Apostle Paul, I came to the place where I was fully convinced that no human being can please God through self-improvement, so I finally trusted Jesus to make me right before God—not myself by trying to be good enough!

I love Galatians 2:19-21 in The Message because it describes my life and testimony perfectly. What actually took place is this: I tried keeping rules and working my head off to please God and it didn't work; so, I gave up the do-do list and began to rest in what Jesus had done for me! Jesus showed me how and **enabled me to do it.** I began to completely identify myself with Jesus: I realized that the old Connie died with Jesus and a brand-new creation rose up with Him. I was one with the King of kings. His perfect righteousness was now my new identity.

When I began to embrace the truth that I was righteous as a gift of grace, my ego was no longer central anymore. It wasn't about what I had done right or wrong. It wasn't about my good works or my great effort to qualify myself, as religion had led me to believe.

All of a sudden, just like these verses describe, it was no longer important what others thought of me. I no longer needed the approval of others, because I was fully approved by my Good Father. I was no longer driven to impress God, because I realized He was fully delighted in me.

Jude 1:24 revealed this powerful truth to me:

"Now to Him Who is able to keep you without stumbling or slipping or falling, and to present [you] unblemished (blameless and faultless) before the presence of His glory in triumphant joy and exultation [with unspeakable, ecstatic delight]" (AMPC).

Your Good Father is already impressed with you! You don't have to follow a list of rules to get His approval. Jesus presents you blameless and faultless in your Father's eyes, and He rejoices over you with unspeakable, ecstatic delight! You are His beloved child and He is fully pleased with you! Jesus showed us how we can live free in the Father's good opinion of us.

In John 8:26 and 54, the religious leaders of the day came against Jesus and had negative opinions about Him, but this is how Jesus responded to their accusations:

"26I say only what I have heard from [my Father] and he is true.

54If I am merely boasting about myself, it doesn't count. But it is my Father who says these glorious things about me" (NLT[1]).

Jesus found peace in the identity He had been given by His Father. And that's what the true Gospel does for us, too. It gives us peace as we live out of our true identities in Christ! We believe what our Good Father says about us. His good opinion is all that matters! He sees no fault in you because of Jesus! (Ephesians 1:4).

I love how The Message Bible ends this beautiful passage of Scripture in Galatians 2:21. If Jesus made us righteous as a free gift—if we are already fully approved, qualified, and accepted in Him—then why would we ever go back to the bondage of peer-pleasing, rule-keeping religion?

I refuse to do that! How about you? Religion says do! Jesus says done! Which message will you embrace?

If we really embrace the identity that Jesus has given us—really receive the truth that we are already approved—would we keep working our heads off for His approval, or for people's approval? If we really received the truth that we were already righteous, would we keep trying to qualify ourselves through religious rules?

No, we wouldn't! We'd finally be free from the religious do-do list. We wouldn't embrace any more messages that pointed to what we needed to do to be blessed, get our prayers answered, or find favor in God's eyes. We would refuse to devalue God's grace, because if being right with God came through rule-keeping, Jesus died for nothing!

But Jesus didn't die for nothing! He died to take away the guilt and shame of our sins and make us perfectly righteous forever. He died to set us free from the fear and condemnation that religious lies have brought to our hearts. He died to prove that you are greatly prized and dearly loved! He rose again to make you one with Him!

Religious rule-keeping has never set anyone free. It only produces pride if you think you are doing it well enough or condemnation if your actions don't measure up. But embracing the true Gospel of Jesus by embracing your true identity in Him produces the beautiful fruit of the Spirit in your life! Who you are on the inside comes out for the whole world to see!

That's what happened to me. When I let go of my do-do list, and rested in what Jesus had done for me, the Holy Spirit brought forth the fruit of righteousness in my life. 2 Corinthians 3:18 says that when we behold Jesus as in a mirror we are transformed into His very image by the power of the Holy Spirit.

Matthew 11:28-30:

> *"28-30Are you tired? Worn out? Burned out on religion? Come to me. Get away with me and you'll recover your life. I'll show you how to take a real rest. Walk with me and work with me—watch how I do it. Learn the unforced rhythms of grace. I won't lay anything heavy or ill-fitting on you. Keep company with me and you'll learn to live freely and lightly"* (MSG).

Oh, the fruit of love, joy, peace, and goodness that comes forth effortlessly in our lives, when we give up our human effort to keep the do-do list and truly begin to trust in what Jesus did for us! He made us righteous and blessed as a pure gift of His grace.

If you've been wearing yourself out, working your head off to please God, it's time to rest! Jesus said, "Has religion burnt you out and brought you to the end of your self-effort? Then come to me!"

Get away with Jesus and you'll recover your life. He will show you how to live from a place of rest in His finished work. Embrace your true identity in Him and you'll learn to live freely and lightly! It's time to break free from the religious lies that have kept you on the hamster wheel of performance-based religion that only produces pride and condemnation in your life. It's time to truly live by embracing your true identity in Christ!

Religion says DO! Jesus says DONE! It's time to experience the freedom that Jesus came to give you!

Galatians 5:1:

> *"Let me be clear, the Anointed One has set us free—not partially, but completely and wonderfully free! We must always cherish this truth and stubbornly refuse to go back into the bondage of religion"* (TPT).

REFLECTION AND DISCUSSION QUESTIONS FOR CHAPTER 8

1. Have you ever been taught you had to "do" something to have God's approval and blessing? What was on your do-do list? Were you ever perfect at doing all those things? There are two ways people respond to the message of performance-based religion:

   a. Try harder

   or

   b. Give up.

   Which way have you responded?

2. What happens when we mingle law (our do-do list) with grace (what Jesus did for us)? What was the "fake gospel" that the Apostle Paul warned us about in Galatians 1:6-7?

3. Discuss what the true Gospel really is. What is the true Gospel that the Apostle Paul taught in Galatians 2:16, 18-21? Does the true Gospel focus on what you need to do or what Jesus has done for you? In Galatians 2:18, what did the Apostle Paul say he would be doing if he taught people they had to follow religious rules to be right with God?

4. Can you relate to how the Apostle Paul describes his former life in Galatians 2:19-21 in The Message Bible? Is it possible to be right before God through obeying the law? If we could be right before God by following religious rules and laws, why did Jesus even need to die?

5. Trying to follow a do-do list of religious rules only produces pride if you think you are doing it well enough or condemnation if your actions don't measure up. But what fruit does believing who you are in Christ produce in your life?

6. Religion says do! Jesus says done! Which message will you embrace?

Chapter 9
Religion Puts You in Bondage! Jesus Sets You Free!

For many years of my Christian life, I believed the lie that Christianity was all about rule-keeping. I accepted Jesus as my Savior when I was a little girl, but for the next twenty years, I thought it was up to me to keep myself saved. There was a long list of rules to follow. I thought that if I followed them, I would be approved by God, and my salvation would be secure.

This lie I believed put me in bondage to rule-keeping, peer-pleasing religion, and eventually left me feeling discouraged and disappointed with my life. This belief of my heart was not working for me. I honestly felt like people who didn't believe in Jesus were happier than I was!

I eventually surrendered my self-effort and thought, *If this is what Christianity is about, I quit!* That's just what Jesus was waiting for!

In Matthew 11:28-30 Jesus said, *"Are you tired? Worn out? Burned out on religion?* **Come to me.** *Get away with me and you'll recover your life. I'll show you how to take a real rest. Walk with me and work with me—watch how I do it. Learn the unforced rhythms of grace. I won't lay anything heavy or ill-fitting on you.* **Keep company with me and you'll learn to live freely and lightly***"* (MSG, emphasis mine).

Wow! What a relief! I could finally quit striving and enter into rest. Jesus said He wouldn't put anything heavy on me. He would teach me to live freely and lightly. After twenty years of living under a heavy load of trying to be good enough through rule-keeping, boy was I ready for that!

Where Did This Lie I Believed Come From? Didn't Jesus Himself Teach Us to Follow Rules?

Several chapters before Jesus said these words in Matthew 11:28-30, He taught a long list of rules. In Matthew chapter 5, Jesus Himself taught about the law in the Sermon on the Mount. In Matthew 5:17, Jesus said, *"If you think I've come to set aside the law of Moses or the writings of the prophets, you're mistaken. I have come to fulfill and bring to perfection all that has been written"* (TPT).

He then proceeded to raise the standard of the law **so high** that everyone listening knew it was impossible for any man to be righteous by trying to keep it. He said in Matthew 5:19, *"So whoever violates even the least important of the commandments, and teaches others to do so, will be the least esteemed in the realm of heaven's kingdom..."* (TPT).

Well I guess that includes all of us! When we are living by our own self-righteousness, we often find ourselves thinking, *I may have done **this**, but at least I didn't do **that**.*

Well, according to Jesus, it doesn't matter. If you break even the smallest commandment, you are guilty of all! (Galatians 3:10).

Jesus went on to say in Matthew 5:21-22:

> *"21You have heard that our ancestors were told, 'You must not murder. If you commit murder, you are subject to judgment.' 22But I say, if you are even angry with someone, you are subject to judgment! If you call someone an idiot, you are in danger of being brought before the court. And if you curse someone, you are in danger of the fires of hell"* (NLT).

Wow! We are all in trouble if that's the end of the story!

In verse 27-28, Jesus said, *"27You have heard the commandment that says, 'You must not commit adultery. 28But I say, anyone who even looks at a woman with lust has already committed adultery with her in his heart"* (NLT). I think Jesus declared all men guilty with that one!

Then in verse 29-30, He says, *"²⁹So if your eye—even your good eye—causes you to lust, gouge it out and throw it away. It is better for you to lose one part of your body than for your whole body to be thrown into hell. ³⁰And if your hand—even your stronger hand—causes you to sin, cut it off and throw it away. It is better for you to lose one part of your body than for your whole body to be thrown into hell"* (NLT). We would all be maimed if we followed that command! I have never met one Christian who ever followed through with that.

In the midst of all of these impossible rules to follow, Jesus went for the jugular. In verses 31-32, He condemned every divorced woman to a life of being alone and unloved by stating that if anyone married her, they were guilty of adultery.

And if that wasn't enough to cause all of us to say, "Uncle," Jesus put the nail in the coffin with this one last command. In verse 48, He said, ***"You are to be PERFECT, even as your Father in heaven is PERFECT!"*** (NLT). Who can possibly do that?

If the purpose in Jesus teaching this sermon was for us to try harder to be righteous by following these commands, we'd all be doomed! No one would be saved because everyone is declared guilty based on the law's demands.

It is interesting to note that when we have a religious mindset, we completely miss the point of what Jesus is trying to teach us in this sermon. We choose which rules we want to follow—the ones we think we are good at.

For example, I've known people who sentenced divorced women to a life of shame and loneliness because of what Jesus said in Matthew 5:31-32, and even refused to attend a second marriage wedding celebration because, **"They were committing adultery."** Yet, these same people would never gouge their eyes out because they had an evil thought about a woman—or a man for that matter! These same people have never acted perfectly, like their Father in heaven is perfect.

Performance-based religion puts people in bondage to self-righteousness or self-condemnation. It only produces judgment in people's hearts based on the law's demands. 2 Corinthians 3:6 tells us that the law condemns and kills, but the Spirit gives us life!

Jesus did teach this long list of impossible rules. But thank God that was not the end of the story! His intention behind this sermon was not for us to try harder to keep the highest standards of the law, but rather to bring us to the end of our self-effort, so we'd give up our self-righteousness for His perfect righteousness.

Jesus actually fulfilled the law for us, took the punishment for all our wrong behavior, and rose again to make us righteous forever. The Good News is that by His one and final sacrifice, He made us perfect forever as a gift of His grace! (Hebrews 10:14).

After this Sermon on the Mount, no wonder Jesus said, "Are you tired? Worn out? Burned out on religion? Then come to Me and I will give you rest!" After hearing that long list of impossible rules to keep, I would think everyone would be ready to say, "I can't do it on my own! I need a Savior!"

Thank you, Jesus! He came, and He rescued us, so we could live free from peer-pleasing, rule-keeping religion, and find true life in Him!

The Truth That Set Me Free!

Romans 10:1-4:

> *"¹Dear brothers and sisters, the longing of my heart and my prayer to God is for the people of Israel to be saved. ²I know what enthusiasm they have for God, but it is misdirected zeal. ³For they don't understand God's way of making people right with himself. Refusing to accept God's way, they cling to their own way of getting right with God by trying to keep the law. ⁴For Christ has already accomplished the purpose for which the law was given. As a result, all who believe in him are made right with God"* (NLT).

> *"⁴For Christ is the end of the law. And because of him, God has transferred his perfect righteousness to all who believe"* (TPT).

Now that's some really Good News! It makes me want to dance and shout! The heavy burden to be made righteous before God through rule-keeping is gone! Jesus fulfilled the law for us! We've been given a brand-new identity that completely fulfills the law. Jesus has given His perfect righteousness to all who believe!

Galatians 2:15-16,19-21:

"15-16...We know very well that we are not set right with God by rule-keeping but only through personal faith in Jesus Christ. How do we know? We tried it— and we had the best system of rules the world has ever seen!

Convinced that no human being can please God by self-improvement, we believed in Jesus as the Messiah so that we might be set right before God by trusting in the Messiah, not by trying to be good.

19-21What actually took place is this: I tried keeping rules and working my head off to please God, and it didn't work. So I quit being a "law man" so that I could be God's man. Christ's life showed me how, and enabled me to do it. I identified myself completely with him.

*Indeed, I have been crucified with Christ. My ego is no longer central. **It is no longer important that I appear righteous before you or have your good opinion**, and I am no longer driven to impress God. Christ lives in me. The life you see me living is not "mine," but it is lived by faith in the Son of God, **who loved me and gave himself for me. I am not going to go back on that.***

> *Is it not clear to you that to go back to that old rule-keeping, peer-pleasing religion would be an abandonment of everything personal and free in my relationship with God? I refuse to do that, to repudiate God's grace. If a living relationship with God could come by rule-keeping, then Christ died unnecessarily"* (MSG, emphasis mine).

These verses make it so clear what the bondage of religion truly is. When we have been given complete acceptance and approval in Christ, to go back to the bondage of peer-pleasing, rule-keeping religion is to abandon everything personal and free in our relationships with Jesus.

Jesus Set You Free From the Bondage of Peer-Pleasing Religion

When we are constantly trying to please everyone, when we are worried about what others think of us, we are still trapped in the spirit of religion. When you can't be led by God's Spirit or follow what's in your heart because you are afraid of someone's disapproval, you are still in bondage to peer-pleasing religion.

I remember a friend of mine telling me that she was afraid to go visit another church because she feared what the leadership of the church she currently attended would think of her if she did. Wow! Now, that's bondage! Have you ever been afraid to follow what was in your heart because you were afraid of what other people might think of you? I know I have!

In John 5:44, Jesus addressed the religious leaders and brought out the fact that they cared more about what others thought then the honor and praise that came from the Father:

> *"How is it possible for you to believe [how can you learn to believe], you who [are content to seek and] receive praise and honor and glory from one another, and yet do not seek the praise and honor and glory which come from Him Who alone is God?"* (AMPC).

Proverbs 29:25:

> *"The fear of human opinion disables; trusting in God protects you from that"* (MSG).

In Matthew 11:28-30, Jesus said, "If you are tired of religion, then learn from Me. Watch how I do it." So, how did Jesus live free from peer-pleasing religion?

In Matthew 3:17, the Father gave His good opinion of Jesus. His true identity was made known:

> *"Then suddenly the voice of the Father shouted from the sky, saying, "This is the Son I love, and my greatest delight is in him""* (TPT).

Then the devil came to tempt Jesus to prove who He was by turning stone into bread, but Jesus replied, *"The Scriptures say: Bread alone will not satisfy, but true life is found in every word, which constantly goes forth from God's mouth"* (Matthew 4:4, TPT).

In this verse, Jesus teaches us, as sons of God, to live from every word our Father says about us. When the religious leaders attacked Jesus with their false opinions and accusations, He simply replied, "I say only what I hear my Father say about me! It's not I who says these glorious things, it's my Father who says them, and what He says about me is true!" (John 8:42-59).

In Jesus, you are already valuable, approved and accepted in Christ—live from that identity! When we live from our Father's good opinion of us, we won't live in fear of what other people think. We are actually free to live from our hearts and be led by God's Spirit.

Jesus lived from the revelation of who He was—that He was His Father's beloved Son and His Father was well-pleased with Him. We see how He lived free from the fear of man, and He has empowered us to live free as well! If we find our lives—our identities—in every word our Father says about us, we'll live free from peer-pleasing religion.

Jesus Set You Free from Rule-Keeping Religion

Jesus hated performance-based religion because it held the ones He loved in bondage to a set of rules which gave them no way of escape. He even said to the religious leaders of the day, "You put heavy weights on people, but you do nothing to help them."

Religion just leaves us in the chains of rule keeping, stuck in our own human effort, chained by the feeling that we will never be good enough! It causes us to feel self-righteous when we think we've been good, and self-condemned when we know we have failed. There is no freedom in the religious system of rule-keeping.

Performance-based religion puts us in bondage to a constant striving for self-improvement instead of living from the truth that we are complete in Christ. If you've been given the perfect righteousness of Jesus Christ, there's no need for self-improvement!

Galatians 4:9-10, 12, 28:

> *"9But now that we truly know him and understand how deeply we're loved by him, why would we, even for a moment, consider turning back to those weak and feeble principles of religion, as though we were still subject to them? 10Why would we want to go backwards into the bondage of religion...?"*
>
> *"12Beloved ones, I plead with you, follow my example and become free from the bondage of religion..."*
>
> *"28Dear friends, just like Isaac, we're now the true children who inherit the kingdom promises"* (TPT).

Galatians 5:1-10:

> *"1Let me be clear, the Anointed One has set us free—not partially, but completely and wonderfully free! We must always cherish this truth and stubbornly refuse to go back into the bondage of our past.*

2I, Paul, tell you: If you think there is benefit in circumcision and Jewish regulations, then you're acting as though Jesus the Anointed One is not enough. **3**I say it again emphatically: If you let yourselves be circumcised you are obliged to fulfill every single one of the commandments and regulations of the law!

4If you want to be made holy by fulfilling the obligations of the law, you have cut off more than your flesh—you have cut yourselves off from the Anointed One and have fallen away from the revelation of grace!

5But the Holy Spirit convinces us that we have received by faith the glorious righteousness of the Anointed One. **6**When you're placed into the Anointed One and joined to him, circumcision and religious obligations can benefit you nothing. All that matters now is living in the faith that is activated and brought to perfection by love.

7Before you were led astray, you were so faithful to Messiah. Why have you now turned away from what is right and true? Who has deceived you?

8The One who enfolded you into his grace is not behind this false teaching that you've embraced. Not at all! **9**Don't you know that when you allow even a *little lie into your heart, it can permeate your entire belief system?*

10Deep in my heart I have faith that the Lord Jesus the Anointed One, who lives in you, will bring you back around to the truth..." (TPT).

Now that we understand that we've been made righteous as a gift of God's grace, and realize how loved we are by Him, why would we ever go back to the bondage of religion? Since Jesus set us free, let's live free, and never go back to trying to be good enough through our obedience to the law.

The Holy Spirit has convinced us that we have received, by faith, the glorious righteousness of Jesus, and the Holy Spirit brings forth the fruit of righteousness in our lives when we believe. When we are in Jesus, religious rules cannot benefit us in any way. All that matters now is living by trusting in Jesus and believing who we are in Him!

You are the righteousness of God in Christ. It's time to break free from peer-pleasing, rule-keeping religion, and live free in your new identity in Him!

REFLECTION AND DISCUSSION
QUESTIONS FOR CHAPTER 9

1. Look at Galatians 2:21 in The Message Bible. What does performance-based religion put us in bondage to?

2. In Matthew 5:17-48, in the sermon on the mount, Jesus showed us the impossibility of trying to be righteous by keeping the law. When you read how Jesus raised the standard of the law to a heart level, which one of His commands brought you to the end of your self-effort? Do we really believe that trying hard to obey will save us?

3. If the sermon on the mount was the end of the story, we'd all be lost in our sin, but what is the Good News about Jesus found in Romans 10:1-4?

4. Have you ever been in bondage to fear of what people think of you? The Apostle Paul described it as peer-pleasing religion. How did Jesus demonstrate to us how we can live a life free from peer-pleasing religion? (Matthew 4:4).

5. Have you ever been in bondage to the fear of not being good enough? The Apostle Paul described this as rule-keeping religion. What did you learn from Galatians 5:1-10? Is it possible to be right before God by rule-keeping? How are you made right with God?

6. Now that you understand how deeply you are loved, and who you are in Christ, why would anyone want to go back to the bondage of peer-pleasing, rule-keeping religion?

7. Freedom is not found in trying to become something, but it is found in realizing who you already are in Christ. How would your life be different if you gave up self-effort for believing who you are in Jesus? What fruit would come forth in your life if you turned your focus from what you need to do to please God to what Jesus did to make you fully accepted, approved, and righteous in your Father's eyes?

8. What if you really believed your Good Father when you heard Him say, "You are my beloved child, whom I dearly love! I am fully pleased with you because of Jesus!" How would it change your whole life?

Chapter 10
Religion Divides Us!
Jesus Made Us One!

Comparison and division are the ultimate deceptions of religion because they are the opposite of love. Religion divides us by our doctrines and our rules. Performance-based religion has divided us into over 40,000 denominations!

When I had a religious mindset, I remember thinking that my denomination was right, and everyone else's was wrong. I can remember the rules that made me separate myself from people. I looked down on people who smoked, drank, or had tattoos. I thought I was better than they were. How self-righteous I was in my thinking! Performance-based religion makes you feel like you're either better than others or not as good as others. It does not produce unity or love.

Galatians 5:4 says, *"If you are trying to make yourselves right with God by keeping the law, you have been cut off from Christ! You have fallen away from God's grace"* (NLT).

This means that anytime religion teaches us that we have to keep rules in order to be righteous before God, it separates us from Christ and ultimately separates us from each other. When we try to be right by our behavior, our church attendance, or our doctrine, it divides us. But when we embrace the gift of being right in God's sight because of Jesus, Jesus makes us one!

The Truth That Set Me Free!

What is the true Gospel of Jesus? What is the message that unites us and makes us one? Jesus prayed for us and revealed that His ultimate mission in being the final sacrifice for us was to make us one in His love.

Jesus Made Us One

In John 17:19, Jesus prayed, *"And I give myself as a holy sacrifice for them **so they can be made holy by your truth**"* (NLT, emphasis mine).

He continued in John 17:20-23, 26:

> *"20And I ask not only for these disciples, but also for all those who will one day believe in me through their message.*
>
> *21I pray for them all to be **joined together as one** even as you and I,*

Father, are joined together as one. **I**
pray for them to become one with
us *so that the world will recognize that*
you sent me.

²²For the very glory you have given to
me I have given them **so that they will**
be joined together as one *and*
experience the same unity that we enjoy.

²³You live fully in me and now I live fully
in them so that they will experience
perfect unity, and the world will be
convinced that you have sent me, for
they will see that you love each one of
them with the same passionate love that
you have for me.

²⁶I have revealed to them who you are
and I will continue to make you even
more real to them, so that they may
experience the same endless love that
you have for me, for your love will now
live in them, even as I live in them!"
(TPT, emphasis mine).

What great love Jesus has for us! He gave us His
very identity as a pure gift of His grace! He said He gave
Himself as a holy sacrifice for you and me so that we
could be made holy. He did this to make us one with
Himself and one with each other.

How did He make us one? Verse 22 says Jesus
made us one by giving us the very same glory the
Father gave to Him. He gave us His glory so that our
hearts would be convinced that each of us is equally

loved by the Father with the same passionate love the Father has for Him.

The word "glory" in verse 22 actually means, "always a good opinion concerning one, resulting in praise, honor, and glory" (Strong's G1391).

So, when Jesus said He gave us the same glory that the Father gave Him, He was saying, "Father, the same good opinion that you have of me, you have of them so that they can live as one in us!

2 Peter 1:17 clearly shows us the glory that the Father gave to Jesus:

> *"He received honor and glory from God the Father* **when the voice came to him from the Majestic Glory, saying, "This is my Son, whom I love; with him I am well pleased"** (NIV, emphasis mine).

This same verse in the Passion Translation says, *"Yes, Father God lavished upon him radiant glory and honor when his distinct voice spoke out of the realm of majestic glory, endorsing him with these words: This is my cherished Son, marked by my love. All my delight is found in him."*

The very same glory the Father gave to Jesus, He has given to you and me! He has the very same good opinion of us as He has of Jesus.

Our Good Father has spoken to us through His Son and said, "You are my beloved child, whom I dearly love! All my delight is found in you! In you, I am well pleased!" WOW! The very same identity He gave to Jesus, He gave to each of us to make us one in Him!

When I was growing up, I used to think my sister was more loved and favored. I compared myself to her and always thought she was better than I was. I was jealous of her because I did not know who I was in Jesus. But when the truth of the Gospel set me free, I realized my sister and I were one in Jesus. I no longer compared myself to her or thought she was better than me because we were equal in Christ. We had the same identity in Jesus!

Jealousy disappeared effortlessly from my heart as I embraced the truth of the Gospel. I was now able to fully love her because I realized I was just as loved and favored as she is because Jesus made us one. What freedom the true Gospel brings to our hearts. It empowers us to truly love each other because He first loved us!

When we live as one in Christ, we get our opinion of ourselves and others from our good Daddy's opinion of us. That's how Jesus lived. Jesus said He only said what His Father said about Him. And His Father said He was His beloved Son in whom He found great delight!

That's how we live. Whatever our Good Father says about us—or our sisters and brothers in Christ—is what we say! When we understand the truth that we are one in Jesus, it brings unity and love to the body of Christ.

However, when we live by rule-keeping religion, we judge each other in the flesh. When I look at you in the flesh, I judge you by your behavior, by your doctrine, or by the church you attend, and it produces division.

But when we look at each other in Christ Jesus, I see that everything about you is beautiful and there is nothing at all wrong with you, and you see the same thing in me (Song of Songs 4:7). I see you equal with Jesus and equal with me.

2 Corinthians 5:16-17 says, *"¹⁶So then, from now on, we have a new perspective that refuses to evaluate people merely by their outward appearances. ¹⁷Now, if anyone is enfolded into Christ, he has become an entirely new creation. All that is related to the old order has vanished. Behold, everything is fresh and new"* (TPT).

We Are Equal in Christ!

Ephesians 2:13-15:

> *"¹³Yet look at you now! Everything is new! Although you were once distant and far away from God, now you have been brought delightfully close to him through the sacred blood of Jesus—**you have actually been united to Christ!***
>
> *¹⁴**Our reconciling "Peace" is Jesus! He has made Jew and non-Jew one in Christ. By dying as our sacrifice, he has broken down every wall of prejudice that separated us and has now made us equal through our union with Christ. ¹⁵Ethnic hatred has been***

dissolved by the crucifixion of his precious body on the cross. *The legal code that stood condemning every one of us has now been repealed by his command..."* (TPT, emphasis mine).

We were made equal through our union with Christ. I'm not better than you, and you're not better than me. Jesus is our peace with each other! He has removed every wall of prejudice and judgment that separated us, by making us one with Him!

Ethnic hatred died! Jesus took away our sin so that we can now see ourselves and others as righteous in Him! The legal code of the law that stood condemning all of us, and caused us to condemn ourselves and judge and condemn each other, has been repealed by His command!

Ephesians 2:15-18:

*"15...**His triune essence has made peace between us** by starting over— forming one new race of humanity, Jews and non-Jews fused together!*

*16Two have now become one, and we live restored to God and reconciled in the body of Christ. **Through his crucifixion, hatred died.** 17For the Messiah has come to preach this sweet message of peace to you, the ones who were distant, and to those who are near. 18**And now, because we are united to Christ, we both have equal and direct access in the realm of the***

> *Holy Spirit to come before the*
> *Father!"* (TPT, emphasis mine).

Isn't that the most beautiful thing you ever heard? Because we are united to Christ, we all have equal access into the realm of the Holy Spirit to come boldly and confidently before our Father. He loves us! He's pleased with us because of Jesus!

For so long religion has lied to us and told us that it is our behavior that makes us pleasing to God. But if that were true, He wouldn't be pleased with any of us because we all fail! By Jesus' final sacrifice, He made us perfectly righteous before the Father forever! And He will never change His good opinion of us! (Hebrews 10:14).

Religion divides us and causes us to judge one another, but Jesus made us one. Could you imagine if we really believed the Gospel that we are one with Jesus? **All who believe the true Gospel live free from ethnic hatred and prejudice.** Jesus put an end to it by making us equal! Our failures can no longer define us! We are defined by our Good Father's opinion of us, and His good opinion of Jesus is His good opinion of us! He has made us one in Christ! We are all equally loved, blessed, righteous, qualified, accepted, and approved because of Jesus!

When the True Gospel is Preached it Produces Unity and Love!

Ephesians 4:5, 11-16:

> *"5For the Lord God is one, and so are we,*
> *for we share in one faith, one baptism,*

and one Father. 6And He is the perfect Father who leads us all, works through us all, and lives in us all!

*11He has appointed some with grace to be apostles, and some with grace to be prophets, and some with grace to be evangelists, and some with grace to be pastors, and some with grace to be teachers. 12And their calling is to nurture and prepare all the holy believers to do their own works of ministry, and as they do this they will enlarge and build up the body of Christ. 13These grace ministries will function until we all attain **oneness in the faith**, until we all experience the fullness of what it means to know the Son of God, and finally we become one perfect man with the full dimensions of spiritual maturity and **fully developed in the abundance of Christ.***

*14**And then our immaturity will end! And we will not be easily shaken by trouble, nor led astray by novel teachings or by the false doctrines of deceivers who teach clever lies.** 15But instead we will remain strong and always sincere in our love as we express the truth. **All our direction and ministries will flow from Christ and lead us deeper into him,** the anointed Head of his body, the church.*

> *16For his "body" has been formed in his image and is closely joined together and constantly connected as one. And every member has been given divine gifts to contribute to the growth of all; and as these gifts operate effectively throughout the whole body, **we are built up and made perfect in love"***
> (TPT, emphasis mine).

I don't know if it could be any clearer. The purpose for our Good Father giving us the ministry of apostles, prophets, evangelists, pastors, and teachers is to build up the body of Christ until we are fully developed in our true identity in Jesus.

When the true Gospel is preached, we are reminded that we are one with Jesus and one with each other! We become fully developed in the abundance of Christ! We are awakened to the truth that we lack nothing in Him! Then immaturity, competition, comparison and division will end! Performance-based religion will no longer be able to deceive us or divide us, but we will be built up and made perfect in His love!

I taught my children when they were growing up that we are The Love Family. Sometimes we may disagree or see things differently. Sometimes we may get upset at each other for a moment, but we always forgive each other. We love each other because Jesus lives in us and He is love. We are one with Love! Jesus loves us and so we love each other, and we accept and approve of each other.

That truth has brought such peace, love and unity in our family. We have had times when one person was tempted to be upset or offended at another, but we always remembered who we are in Jesus. We are One in Him! We are The Love Family, because He is Love!

What would happen if the body of Christ was taught that we are The Love Family because we are one with love? It would produce unity and love among us! We would know our true identity in Jesus!

Colossians 1:25-29:

> *"25God has given me the responsibility of serving his church by proclaiming his entire message to you. 26This message was kept secret for centuries and generations past, but now it has been revealed to God's people. 27For God wanted them to know that the riches and glory of Christ are for you Gentiles, too. And this is the secret: Christ lives in you.* **This gives you assurance of sharing his glory**" (NLT, emphasis mine).

> *"28-29***Christ is our message!** *We preach to awaken hearts and bring every person into the full understanding of truth. It has become my inspiration and passion in ministry to labor with a tireless intensity, with his power flowing through me, to present to every believer the revelation of being his perfect one in Jesus Christ"* (TPT, emphasis mine).

Wow! If we are not preaching that Jesus lives in us and we share His glory, if Jesus isn't the focus of every message we preach, if we are not awaking hearts to bring our brothers and sisters in Christ into the full understanding that they are His perfect one in Christ, then we are not preaching the Gospel!

Performance-based religion does not focus on Jesus. It focuses on man's self-effort. It focuses on what man needs to do to please God. It does not awaken hearts to our true identities in Jesus, but rather teaches rules that we must follow to try to be righteous. This is not the true Gospel. When the focus of our message is man's performance, it produces division, separation and destruction in the body of Christ.

Like the Apostle Paul, when the apostle, prophet, evangelist, pastor, and teacher is passionate about awakening hearts to their true identities in Jesus and reminding them that they are one in Him, immaturity will end. Division will end! Competition will end! Jealousy will end! Comparison will end! Jesus will be our focus, which will produce in us unity and love!

Can you imagine if every church in every city came together for one purpose, one faith, and one reason to build each other up in the love of Jesus and our identities in Him? Could you imagine the impact we would make on the world if our focus was Jesus and not ourselves?

There would be no more judgment, no more condemnation, and no more accusing each other. We would love each other because He first loved us! We wouldn't be deceived by any messages that divide us or separate us from Jesus and one another.

Ephesians 4:5-16 teaches us that when we understand the abundance that we have in Christ we will remain strong and sincere, as we express the truth in love. Verse 15 says that all our direction and ministries will flow from Christ and lead us deeper into Him. When the true Gospel is preached, Jesus is the focus of every message!

Division, jealousy, competition, comparing ourselves to each other, and arguing over doctrine is a religious mindset. It's the result of living our lives focused on ourselves instead of Jesus!

1 Corinthians 3:3-4, 16:

> "*3For you are living your lives dominated by the mind-set of the flesh. Ask yourselves: Is there jealousy among you? Do you compare yourselves with others? Do you quarrel like children and end up taking sides? If so, **this proves that you are living your lives centered on yourselves**, dominated by the mind-set of the flesh, and behaving like unbelievers. 4For when you divide yourselves up in groups—a "Paul group" and an "Apollos group"— you're acting like people without the Spirit's influence*" (TPT, emphasis mine).

> "*16Don't you realize that all of you together are the temple of God and that the Spirit of God lives in you?*" (NLT).

This passage of Scripture so clearly teaches that when we divide ourselves over doctrine, we are acting like unbelievers. We have been deceived by performance-based religion and, therefore, still attempting to make ourselves right by something other than Jesus.

But listen to the sweet sound of correction in verse 16. If we are experiencing jealousy, or if we find ourselves comparing or arguing over doctrine, the Holy Spirit reminds us that all of us together are the temple of God and the Spirit of God lives in us! We are one in Christ!

So if you're ever tempted to be jealous, to condemn, to judge, or to accuse one of your brothers or sisters in Christ—if you're ever tempted to reject one of your brothers or sisters in Christ because they believe differently then you or hold a different doctrine than you—remember, that comes from a religious mindset that is focused on yourself instead of Jesus.

Turn your eyes back to Jesus and remember who you are. You are one with the King of kings! You are righteous. You are loved. You are just like Jesus and so is your brother and sister in Christ. We live free from a religious mindset and live with a mind controlled by the Spirit. We don't look at each other in the flesh. We look at each other in the spirit, and we remember that when we look at each other, we're looking at Jesus.

I want to end this chapter with a prayer:

Heavenly Father, thank You for showing us how much You love us. Thank You for sending Jesus to make us one so that we no longer have to live in the bondage of division, separation, jealousy, comparison and competition. We no longer have to try to be right by our behavior or our doctrine because we are already perfectly righteous in Jesus! Father, you have made us one with you and one with each other. Give us a deeper revelation of that truth so that we can live in the freedom that Jesus came to give us, loving ourselves, loving each other, and living in the freedom of Your love. Thank You for showing us the truth that sets us free! In Jesus Name! Amen!

REFLECTION AND DISCUSSION
QUESTIONS FOR CHAPTER 10

1. How does performance-based religion divide us? How does Jesus make us one?

2. According to Galatians 5:4, what teaching separates us from Christ and each other?

3. Right before Jesus laid His life down for each of us, what did He pray for us all? What did Jesus give us to make us one? How can we experience perfect unity in Jesus?

4. Jesus said He gave you and I the very same glory that the Father gave Him. What was the glory the Father gave Jesus and how does that make us all equal in Christ. (2 Peter 1:17).

5. According to 2 Corinthians 5:16-17, how are we to view each other? How does this make us one?

6. Explain the truth found in Ephesians 2:13-17. How did Jesus destroy the wall of prejudice and judgment that separated us?

7. When the true Gospel is preached, it produces unity and love. What is the calling of every ministry? (Ephesians 4:12-13). When we are teaching the true Gospel, what will all our messages flow from and lead us deeper into? (Ephesians 4:15). What will focusing on Jesus produce in the body of Christ? (Ephesians 4:16).

8. What did the Apostle Paul say was the true message of the Gospel? What was the message he was passionate about sharing? (Colossians 1:25-29).

9. According to 1 Corinthians 3:3-5, what is the result of a message that is focused on our performance instead of Jesus? Can you see division, competition, and comparison in the church today? What is the answer? How can we truly live as one in Jesus?

About the Author

Connie Witter is a speaker, author, and Bible study teacher. Her best-selling book, *P.S. God Loves You*, has sold over 200,000 copies. She is the founder of Because of Jesus Ministries, which was established in 2006. Her best-selling Bible study, *Because of Jesus*, was published in 2002 and is the foundation of her life and ministry.

Connie has traveled throughout the United States and internationally, sharing the life-changing message of *Because of Jesus*. She has been the guest speaker at churches, men and women's conferences, ladies retreats and meetings, and has also spoken into the lives of teenagers. She has been a guest on several Christian TV and radio programs, and has had her own nationwide weekly TV program, *Because of Jesus, with Connie Witter*.

Her online Bible studies can be seen worldwide through her ministry website www.conniewitter.com, and her social media pages. Many of her Bible study series can be found on sound cloud.

Thousands of lives have been changed through her ministry. If you are interested in having Connie come speak at your event, you can contact her at:

Connie@conniewitter.com

Other Books by Connie Witter

Bible Studies:

Because of Jesus
Living Loved, Living Free
Awake to Righteousness Volume 1
Awake to Righteousness Volume 2

Books:

Living Loved Living Free
P.S. God Loves You
21 Days to Discover Who You Are in Jesus

For Teens and Children:

The Inside Story—Teen Devotional
The Inside Story for Girls—Devotional
Are You a Chicken Head? I Believe What Jesus Says!—
Children's book
Yes I Am!—Preschool Curriculum

You can purchase any of these resources at:
www.BecauseofJesus.com

We would love to hear how this book impacted your life!

To Contact the author, write:

Connie Witter
Because of Jesus Ministries
PO Box 3064
Broken Arrow, OK 74013-3064

Or Email Connie at:
Connie@conniewitter.com

For additional copies of this book go to:
www.conniewitter.com
or call 918-994-6500